PAGAN MYTH AND CHRISTIAN
TRADITION IN ENGLISH POETRY

CHOICE   OCT. '69

Language & Literature

English & American

BUSH, Douglas. **Pagan Myth and Christian Tradition in English Poetry. American Philosophical Society, 1968. 112p bibl (Jayne Lectures for 1967/Memoirs of the American Philosophical Society, 72) 68-8639. 2.50**
Although occasionally overlapping the content of Bush's widely read works on mythology (*Mythology and the Renaissance Tradition in English Poetry*, rev. ed., 1963; *Mythology and the Romantic Tradition in English Poetry*, 1937), this volume is not a summary of them. Pagan myth and Christian tradition are surveyed in English poetry of "The Renaissance," "The Romantic Revival," and "The Modern Period." Because the text of the book was presented as the Jayne Lectures for 1967, Bush has restricted his considerations to myths and traditions that appear most often in the works of major poets of these periods. He has, however, documented his text with notes that lead the interested reader deeply into the subject matter. Index; useful bibliography.

MEMOIRS OF THE

AMERICAN PHILOSOPHICAL SOCIETY

Held at Philadelphia
For Promoting Useful Knowledge
Volume 72

PAGAN MYTH

AND

CHRISTIAN TRADITION

IN

ENGLISH POETRY

DOUGLAS BUSH

Gurney Professor of English Literature, Emeritus
Harvard University

Jayne Lectures for 1967

AMERICAN PHILOSOPHICAL SOCIETY
INDEPENDENCE SQUARE • PHILADELPHIA

1968

The Jayne Lectures of the American Philosophical Society honor the memory of Henry La Barre Jayne, 1857-1920, a distinguished citizen of Philadelphia and an honored member of the Society. They perpetuate in this respect the aims of the American Society for the Extension of University Teaching, in which Mr. Jayne was deeply interested. When in 1946 this organization was dissolved, having in large measure fulfilled its immediate purposes, its funds were transferred to the American Philosophical Society, which agreed to use them "for the promotion of university teaching, including *inter alia* lectures, publications and research in the fields of science, literature, and the arts."

Accepting this responsibility, the Society initiated in 1961 a series of lectures to be given annually or biennially by outstanding scholars, scientists, and artists, and to be published in book form by the Society. The lectures are presented at various cultural institutions of Philadelphia. Thus far the following, including the series published in the present volume, have been presented:

For
GEOFFREY AND SUKIE

Foreword

While classic myth is often fused with all the other elements that make up poetry, and indeed all forms of literature, there is virtue in separating it for consideration so that critics and literary historians and indeed the cultivated reader may appreciate and appraise the part that it has in the products of the imagination. It is substance, ornament, and catalyst. And as Dr. Bush says, it is well to view its function at different times and over a long period of time. In this way its ebb and flow can be seen and its total contribution recognized. That contribution has been continuous throughout post-classical times, and its importance as a source of inspiration has been great.

In selecting this aspect of literature for his series of Jayne Lectures, Dr. Bush has done what the committee rather expected him to do when it invited him to deliver the 1967 lectures. Ever since his undergraduate days at Toronto and his concentration on the classical languages and literatures in college, he has had a consuming interest in the impact of those literatures and of the great myths which they embody. His Ph.D. dissertation at Harvard was on one aspect of the subject and formed the basis of his first book, *Mythology and the Renaissance Tradition in English Poetry*. This was followed in due time by *Mythology and the Romantic Tradition in English Poetry*, and other books reflecting his preoccupation with the theme. Professor Bush remarks that in preparing the present lectures he proceeded on the assumption that those who would hear them read or who would read them in their published form would not have read the two volumes in which he explored the subject in depth. Such a statement is characteristically modest. Both books have been widely read and have been bought by those who like to own the books they like. Both have had to be reissued twice, the earlier volume in revised form.

It would be a mistake to suppose, however, that the present lectures are but a distillation of the earlier books, useful as such a distillation would be. Their scope is wider and they contain much that is new. What is more, Professor Bush has

vii

taken the opportunity which they afforded of presenting his subject in fresh perspective. It is hoped that the charm and grace with which they were presented will carry over, as I believe it does, to those who were not so fortunate as to hear them delivered.

ALBERT C. BAUGH

Author's Preface

It is too late to express regret for what seems to be an incurable instinct for treating in a few lectures a subject that requires a few volumes. And I am not sure that I feel much regret. As special studies of poets, periods, and topics multiply far beyond the assimilative capacity of literary specialists, even specialists in this or that area, there may be warrant for an occasional small book that is not addressed to departments of English and does not seek to enlarge specialists' knowledge. There is, I think, a modest satisfaction to be gained from a short view of a long stretch of time and a large body of material, even if the various segments of that time and material are more or less familiar, since the suggestive facts of continuity and change are recognizable only in a full perspective.

The use of classical myth in the poetry of several countries and many centuries, and the interpretative and critical theories that have attended it, have been described and analyzed in many books, but these, even the larger ones, are inevitably confined to particular countries or periods or poets or myths, are fragments of an actual whole. A comprehensive survey of the poetry of all countries would be of encyclopedic bulk and would have to be done by international committees. One important fact is that such an ideal history would take in most of the world's great poets from antiquity to the present. Another is that the long story is not a closed chapter or book, a subject of merely historical interest (not that great poetry ever comes under that heading). At first thought classical myth looks very remote from our world, which so often seems intent upon rejecting the whole past; yet it continues, reinterpreted as always, to be an active element in modern literature, stimulated by but not dependent upon the modern interest in "myth" in the broad anthropological sense. If classical myth has in recent decades been in much less common use than formerly, it would still yield a notable anthology of poems and passages and would include some of the greatest names; it supplied the framework for the chief modern novel in English, *Ulysses*;

and it has been conspicuous in drama, opera, and ballet. Most of the leading writers of contemporary France, especially in the drama, have put myth to signal use—Valéry, Claudel, Gide, Giraudoux, Camus, Cocteau, Sartre, Anouilh. We may think of themes and methods as far apart as those of Rilke and Kazantzakis' *Odyssey*.[1] (Whether myth continues to inspire sculpture and painting I cannot say; it may have succumbed to compositions of wire, tin cans, optical charts, and blobs of paint—all embraced within the primeval myth of Chaos. And a number of American novelists have given unwearied and not unrewarded devotion to Priapus.)

For various reasons classical myth has been less attractive to modern American poets, major and minor, apart from the Europeanized pioneers of modernism, Eliot and Pound. One large reason may be conscious or unconscious obedience to Whitman's injunction *(Song of the Exposition)*:

Come Muse migrate from Greece and Ionia,
Cross out please those immensely overpaid accounts,
That matter of Troy and Achilles' wrath, and Æneas', Odysseus' wanderings,
Placard "Removed" and "To Let" on the rocks of your snowy Parnassus . . . .
For know a better, fresher, busier sphere, a wide, untried domain awaits, demands you.

However, in the latter half of the nineteenth century many American poets and versifiers, Longfellow and Lowell and a swarm of the less familiar, declined to leave Greece and Ionia. Emerson, as we might expect, had his own vitalistic conceptions of Pan and Bacchus. In the first decade of our century

---

[1]In addition to studies of the authors named, and general books on modern drama (e.g., those of John Gassner) , some more special surveys are: H. J. Mason, "Classical Myth in Modern Drama," *Emory University Quarterly* 10 (1954) : pp. 256-265; E. Ludovicy, "Le Mythe grec dans le théâtre français contemporain," *Revue des Langues Vivantes* 22 (1956) : pp. 387-418; C. D. Perry, "Classical Myth in Grand Opera," *Classical Journal* 53 (1957-1958) : pp. 207-213; Louise Bogan, review of the *Larousse Encyclopedia of Mythology, The New Yorker*, February 6, 1960; M. O. Lee, "Orpheus and Eurydice: Some Modern Versions," *Classical Journal* 56 (1960-1961) : pp. 307-313; W. Ramsey, "The *Oresteia* since Hoffmannsthal: Images and Emphases," *RLC* 38 (1964) : pp. 359-375, on French and American writers (with references) . See also M. J. Friedman, *"Amphitryon 38:* Some Notes on Jean Giraudoux and Myth," and— along with the books on Rilke—Ralph Freedman, "Gods, Heroes, and Rilke," both essays in *Hereditas*, ed. F. Will (Austin, 1964) .

a cluster of mythological dramas came from three scholarly poets, Trumbull Stickney, William Vaughn Moody, and George Cabot Lodge. In treating Prometheus, Moody, in contrast to the rather grim Stickney, carried on the Romantic theme of the divine fire of abundant life. During the first three decades almost every writer, from Edith Wharton to the author of the *Spoon River Anthology*, produced his or her quota of mythological poems. Romantic Hellenism appeared in a new Imagist disguise in the volumes of "H. D." Robinson Jeffers, the violent primitivist who sought "to uncenter the human mind from itself,"[2] utilized the myths of the *Oresteia* and Medea; and Eugene O'Neill rewrote the *Oresteia* in terms of Freud and New England. Meanwhile Eliot and Pound had been setting poetry on a new course, and they and Yeats were revivifying both "myth" and mythology for both English and American poets.

If modern poets have made less use of mythology than their predecessors, some general reasons are that the post-Romantic tradition had become anaemic, that mythology is a less central and instinctive part of the modern writer's cultural and imaginative equipment, and that poets have more or less shared a modern distrust of everything except the data of immediate experience and have made their "myths" out of those. But while the modern outlook is usually rationalistic and naturalistic, the decisive thing is the temperament of the writer; and the common erosion of religious faith may help either to lessen or to strengthen the appeal of classical myth. I mentioned Emerson's *Bacchus*, a buoyant product of New England Transcendentalism; the *Bacchus* of the violently anti-Christian William Empson[3] is an intellectual network which (with the author's copious notes) yields none of the Romantic intoxications of Emerson—or D. H. Lawrence. Of one major American poet a critic says, summing up the negative side of many poems and much criticism: "This vanishing of the gods, leaving a barren man in a barren land, is the basis of all Stevens'

2A letter of Jeffers' quoted by Lawrence C. Powell, *An Introduction to Robinson Jeffers* (Dijon, 1932), pp. 196-197; *cf.* Frederic I. Carpenter, *Robinson Jeffers* (New York, 1962), pp. 49-54, 69-72, 109 f.

3William Empson, *Bacchus* (*Collected Poems* (London, 1955), pp. 42-45). The author's notes occupy pp. 104-110.

thought and poetry"; to quote one of the poet's own utterances, "the integrations of the past" have become a mere "Museo Olimpico."[4] In the terms of Stevens' most famous poem, *Sunday Morning*, man's craving for the transcendental, for a bond between the human and the divine, was once fulfilled by pagan and Christian beliefs, but such fantasies are now dead; man and life and earth embody whatever divinity or heaven there is. Stevens looked back on the poem as "simply an expression of paganism."[5] Yet another pagan poet, more receptive toward the mythic and supernatural, could realize the union of a god and a mortal with the concrete force of *Leda and the Swan*.

Classical myths are still a potent resource for very diverse poets, notably four who will be our chief modern concern, the non-Christian or anti-Christian Yeats and Pound and the Christian Eliot and Edwin Muir. And there have been recent American plays. William Alfred in *Agememnon* (1954) reinterpreted with originality and power the ancient theme of wrong and retribution. Even Tennessee Williams transposed a myth into his own key and costume (*Orpheus Descending*, 1958).[6] Since these lectures were written, Robert Lowell has reworked *Prometheus Bound* in prose and Archibald MacLeish the murderous madness of Heracles treated by Euripides and Seneca;[7] both writers have invested the myths with modern ethical and metaphysical questionings, Lowell within the original Aeschylean frame, MacLeish by providing a modern figure parallel to Heracles. With these and other examples before us, we can probably assume that classical myths will continue to be available and essential, even in our world of science and violence,

---

4J. Hillis Miller, *Poets of Reality: Six Twentieth-Century Writers* (Cambridge, Mass., Harvard University Press, 1965), p. 219. The phrases following, from Wallace Stevens (*Collected Poems* (New York, Alfred A. Knopf, 1955), p. 342), are quoted by Miller on the same page.

5*Letters of Wallace Stevens*, ed. Holly Stevens (New York, Alfred A. Knopf, 1966), p. 250 (a letter of March 31, 1928, to L. W. Payne, Jr.). *Sunday Morning* was written in 1915.

6William Alfred's *Agamemnon* (1954) was published by Alfred A. Knopf. Tennessee Williams' *Orpheus Descending* (Norfolk, Conn., 1958: revised from *Battle of Angels*, 1940) is reprinted in *Best American Plays: Fifth Series 1957-1963*, ed. John Gassner (New York, 1963).

7Robert Lowell, *Prometheus Bound, derived from Aeschylus*, first printed in *The New York Review of Books*, July 13, 1967; Archibald MacLeish, *Herakles: a play in verse* (Boston, Houghton Mifflin, 1967).

for the same reason that has kept them alive through so many skeptical and troubled centuries—that no newly minted images and symbols can take their place—at least until "Universal Darkness buries All."

Many years ago I wrote two fairly fat volumes on the mythological tradition in English poetry which have been reprinted and continue to sell but are here assumed to have been unread. The present lectures are not, however, merely a summary of those books; they deal with three phases of one special theme, a theme which has been more or less active through nearly twenty centuries of European culture. In spite of the limits of space it seemed better to be selective and specific than comprehensive and abstract. A good many bits were omitted when the lectures were delivered. The notes and bibliography go somewhat beyond the scope of the text, but they too are necessarily very limited, since a full apparatus would sink this small craft; such ballast may, though, have its uses.

I am indebted, as always, to the staff of the Harvard libraries, and also to the hospitality of the Dartmouth College Library and the Boston Public Library.

I am very grateful to the American Philosophical Society for the honor of being invited to give the Jayne Lectures for 1967, and in particular to Dr. George W. Corner, Executive Officer of the Society, and Dr. Emerson Greenaway, head of the Free Library of Philadelphia. These gentlemen made all things gracious and agreeable for my wife and me. Dr. Albert C. Baugh's very friendly Foreword to this book revives the memory of the cordial entertainment we received from him and Mrs. Baugh and from other members of the Department of English of the University of Pennsylvania. I have also a pleasant memory of the people who resisted the temptation to spend one or two or three evenings elsewhere, and who listened with the attentive interest that cheers a lecturer's heart.

D. B.

Cambridge, Massachusetts

Acknowledgments

I am much obliged to the following publishers for permission to quote from copyright books:

Faber and Faber (London), for quotations from T. S. Eliot's *Collected Poems*, the prose notes to *The Waste Land*, and *Notes towards the Definition of Culture*; Edwin Muir's *Collected Poems*; *The Letters of Ezra Pound*, ed. D. D. Paige, and Pound's *Personae*; and Wallace Stevens' *Collected Poems, Letters*, ed. H. Stevens, and *Opus Posthumous*, ed. S. F. Morse.

Harcourt, Brace, & World, Inc. (New York), for quotations from T. S. Eliot's *Complete Poems and Plays*, the prose notes to *The Waste Land*, and *Notes towards the Definition of Culture*; and *The Letters of Ezra Pound*, ed. D. D. Paige.

Alfred A. Knopf (New York), for quotations from Wallace Stevens' *Collected Poems, Letters*, ed. H. Stevens, and *Opus Posthumous*, ed. S. F. Morse.

A. P. Watt and Son and Mr. M. B. Yeats and Macmillan and Company, Ltd. (London), and The Macmillan Company (New York) for quotations from W. B. Yeats's *Autobiographies, Essays and Introductions*, and *A Vision*, and for quotations reprinted with permission of The Macmillan Company from *Collected Poems* by William Butler Yeats. Copyright 1903, 1906, 1907, 1912, 1916, 1918, 1919, 1924, 1928, 1931, 1933, 1934, 1935, 1940, 1944, 1945, 1946, 1950, 1956 by The Macmillan Company.

New Directions, for the quotation from *Hugh Selwyn Mauberley*, in *Personae*, copyright 1926 by Ezra Pound: permission New Directions Publishing Corporation, New York.

Oxford University Press (New York), for quotations from Edwin Muir's *Collected Poems* and W. B. Yeats's introduction to *The Oxford Book Of Modern Verse*.

Twayne Publishers (New York), for the quotation from D. H. Lawrence's *A Propos of Lady Chatterley's Lover*.

Contents

Abbreviations Used in Notes and Bibliography

Bush, *Renaissance Tradition*. See Bibliography, I, below.

Bush, *Romantic Tradition*. See Bibliography, II, below.

CL = Comparative Literature

ELH = ELH: A Journal of English Literary History

JEGP = Journal of English and Germanic Philology

JWCI = Journal of the Warburg and Courtauld Institutes

MLN = Modern Language Notes

MLR = Modern Language Review

MP = Modern Philology

PMLA = Publications of the Modern Language Association of America

RES = Review of English Studies

RLC = Revue de Littérature Comparée

SEL = Studies in English Literature

Seznec. See Bibliography, I, below.

SP = Studies in Philology

Starnes and Talbert. See Bibliography, I, below.

UTQ = University of Toronto Quarterly.

In the footnotes and bibliography the conventions are those preferred by the American Philosophical Society.

PAGAN MYTH AND CHRISTIAN TRADITION IN ENGLISH POETRY

I. *The Renaissance*

I N OUR TIME anthropology and psychology have given a very
broad meaning to the word "myth" as connoting any story that
embodies an experience, theme, ritual, or vision that is in
essence timeless and universal and invites continual re-creation,
conscious or unconscious: thus the word may be used of
Coleridge's *Ancient Mariner* or Faulkner's *The Bear*.[1] Our
present concern is myth in the stricter sense of the body of
Greek and Roman myths which have been an immemorial part
of the Western cultural tradition and have been used with infinite diversity in literature, painting, sculpture, and music.
Our survey of a long tract of time and an immense mass of
material will, though limited to poetry in English, necessarily
touch only some major writers and themes, and those briefly;
but we may hope to see a fairly coherent pattern of both continuity and change. While our concern with sophisticated
literary uses of myth happily frees us from much-debated problems of origins, one general fact may be stressed at the outset:
in ancient as well as later times Greek and Roman myth was
not a body of fixed data but was always evolving, often con-
fusedly and contradictorily, acquiring new embellishments and
new meanings. When, for instance, the Greek writers of
tragedy took up Homeric and other stories, they molded them
afresh in accordance with their own dramatic, philosophical,
and religious ideas. And later poets have continually done like-

---

[1]The simple sentence in the text may serve to suggest the modern literary
concern with archetypal myth familiarly represented by the writings of Maud
Bodkin, Northrop Frye, Stanley E. Hyman, Herbert Weisinger, Philip Wheel-
wright, and many others. There are also the anthropologists and folklorists,
less directly involved with literature, who have studied the origins and
development of ritual, myth, and related phenomena. In the many-sided exposition and debate Greek and Roman myth has naturally had a conspicuous
place, but, the scope and size of this book being what they are, it has not
seemed necessary to include such materials in the notes or bibliography.

1

wise: witness Dante's episode of Ulysses' final voyaging into the
unknown West, and countless other examples we shall meet
along our way.

We may first take account of the general climate that enabled pagan myth to be transplanted and to flourish through
the many Christian centuries. In its beginnings Christianity
itself assimilated elements of pagan religion and thought, and,
after the first clashes between the new and the old faiths,
Christian civilization recognized that in all its secular activities,
and even in its moral life, it had much to learn from the
ancients. Then Latin was the language of learning and the
professions, and of the universal church, the heir of the Roman
empire, and all students of classical Latin necessarily absorbed
classical mythology. But the supreme and all-embracing motive,
at its height during the Renaissance, was the universal reverence felt for the ancients as a superior race and for the moral
wisdom, of almost Christian elevation, to be found in such
thinkers as Cicero and to be extracted even from comedy and
satire. Along with that, of course, went emulous admiration for
the classical poets as imaginative masters of art and style.

More special feelings and modes of thought contributed to
the assimilation and familiar use of mythology. There was, first,
its intrinsic vitality and fascination. Various added attractions,
simple or subtle, were powerful too. For the ancient Greeks,
Homer was a sort of Bible, and, as Plato's *Republic* reminds
us, the behavior of Homer's gods and goddesses could arouse
misgivings. But, as Plato also reminds us, allegorical interpretation had already come to the rescue of religion and morality.[2]
The allegorical method, carried on into the Christian era, was
for many centuries a strong and adaptable agent for reinter-
preting first the dubiously moral or miraculous incidents in

2Plato, *Republic* ii. 377-383, iii. 386-392; *cf. Phaedrus* 229B-230A and *Ion.*
Some references are: Anne B. Hersman, *Studies in Greek Allegorical Inter-
pretation* (Chicago, 1906); Fritz Wehrli, *Zur Geschichte der allegorischen
Deutung Homers im Altertum* (Borna-Leipzig, 1928); J. Tate, *Classical Review*
41 (1927): pp. 214-215, *Classical Quarterly* 23 (1929): pp. 41-45, 142-154, *ibid.*
24 (1930), pp. 1-10; Roger Hinks, *Myth and Allegory in Ancient Art*, H.
Rahner, *Greek Myths and Christian Mystery*, and E. R. Curtius, *European
Literature and the Latin Middle Ages* (pp. 203-246, etc.), all three cited below,
Bibliography, General and I.

the Bible and then the myths and tales narrated by the pagan poets. Early in the sixth century Fulgentius compiled a long-lived dictionary of allegorized mythology and also turned the *Aeneid* into a kind of pilgrim's progress; in the latter work we may feel that, apart from his flat-footed literalness, the interpreter's instinct was not altogether wrong. Then in his fourth eclogue Virgil had associated a new golden age of peace in Italy with the birth of a wondrous child, and throughout the Middle Ages the poem was taken as a prophecy of the birth of Christ. These and other reasons gave Virgil a unique preeminence, so that Dante could take the purest and loftiest of Roman poets as his first guide on his imaginary journey. And, as he began that journey, the Christian allegorist could say, with full awareness of a difference but with no disturbing sense of incongruity: "I am not Aeneas, I am not Paul" (*Inferno* ii. 32).

Even the myths of Ovid's *Metamorphoses* could be interpreted by medieval allegorists in religious as well as in moral, euhemeristic, and cosmological terms. Thus Pyramus is Christ, Thisbe is the human soul, the wall between them is sin, the lion is the devil, the fountain is the baptismal font, the mulberry tree is the Cross.[3] This neat equation is equally far from Ovid's pathetic romance and from the play acted by Bottom and his fellows, but it is not a bit wilder than many recent interpretations of literature by free-wheeling practitioners of Freudian or myth-and-symbol criticism. The chief medieval

---

[3]The religious interpretation of Pyramus is from *Metamorphosis ovidiana Moraliter a Magistro Thoma Walleys . . . explanata* (Paris, 1509), fol. xxxvi*. This book, which had a number of editions, was the work of the fourteenth-century Petrus Berchorius (Pierre Bersuire), a friend of Petrarch. See F. Ghisalberti, "L' 'Ovidius Moralizatus' di Pierre Bersuire," *Studi Romanzi* 23 (1933): pp. 5-136; J. Seznec (Bibliography, I, below); E. H. Wilkins, "Descriptions of Pagan Divinities from Petrarch to Chaucer," *Speculum* 32 (1957): pp. 511-522; E. Panofsky, *Renaissance and Renascences* (Stockholm, 1960), pp. 78-81, n. 2. On Shakespeare's burlesque and earlier, serious versions of the tale, see Madeleine Doran, "Pyramus and Thisbe Once More," *Essays on Shakespeare and Elizabethan Drama in Honor of Hardin Craig*, ed. Richard Hosley (Columbia, Mo., 1962), pp. 149-161.

In addition to Seznec, some references for the allegorizing of mythology in the Middle Ages are given in the Bibliography, I, below: see L. K. Born, J. D. Cooke, W. C. Curry, E. R. Curtius, R. H. Green, F. Munari, E. Panofsky, R. Tuve.

compilation of allegorized mythology was that of Boccaccio, which worked on different principles from his *Decameron*; it held first place until the middle of the sixteenth century. Then and later came new dictionaries of mythology which were somewhat more sophisticated and dealt in moral and cosmological rather than religious interpretations; and, while uncritically and unclassically syncretic, they were convenient works of reference and were richer than their predecessors in iconographical data and excerpts from the classical poets.[4] Such books, intended especially for poets and painters, were used all over Europe, and for such symbolists as Spenser, George Chapman, and Ben Jonson they had the value *The Golden Bough* has had for modern writers. Allegorical interpretation—which did not at all preclude aesthetic enjoyment—was one large and lasting way of reconciling pagan myth with Christianity; it was in full accord with traditional reverence for ancient wisdom. And that reverence permitted the occasional comic use of myth, as in Shakespeare.

Another mode of reconciliation, which developed especially among Italian Neoplatonists of the fifteenth century, might be called an approach to comparative religion: the idea that pagan myths were garbled versions of Biblical truth and hence in their way acceptable in themselves and as evidence of universal validity. The wars of the Giants and Titans against the gods suggested the revolt of Satan and his fellows against God and their imprisonment in hell. The myth of a primitive golden age[5] giving way to progressive corruption naturally linked it-

---

4The chief sixteenth-century mythographers were three Italians, Lilio Gregorio Giraldi, Natale Conti (Natalis Comes), and Vincenzo Cartari. The best account of them and of the whole allegorical tradition is given by J. Seznec (below, Bibliography, I). See also *(ibid.)* D. Bush, D. T. Starnes and E. W. Talbert, and Madeleine Doran's "Some Renaissance 'Ovids,'" a succinct description of five ways of reading the *Metamorphoses;* and some of the following notes.

5On the Golden Age see *The Earthly Paradise and the Renaissance Epic* (Princeton, 1966), pp. 15-33, by A. Bartlett Giamatti, who gives abundant references; A. O. Lovejoy and G. Boas, *Primitivism and Related Ideas in Antiquity* (Baltimore, 1935); Harry Levin, "The Golden Age and the Renaissance," *Literary Views,* ed. Carroll Camden (Chicago, 1964), and *The Myth of the Golden Age in the Renaissance* (forthcoming).

self with Eden and the Fall. There was an obvious parallel, as Milton noted, between Eve and Pandora.[6] Ovid's tale of a great flood and the survival of one righteous husband and wife was clearly an approximation to the story of Noah. A less edifying item was the equating of Noah—because of his getting drunk— with Bacchus, an equation assisted, in an age of untrammeled etymological guessing, by a supposed identity of names.[7] Apart from such theorizing, perhaps nothing in the process of Christian assimilation is more simple and striking than the Latin version of the Lord's Prayer in that Bible of generations of English schoolboys, William Lily's Latin Grammar: "Our Father who art in heaven" becomes *O Pater omnipotens, clarique habitator Olympi.*

A similar approach to myth was offered by typology, with which most educated Christians were necessarily familiar. Just as various prominent figures in the Old Testament, Joshua for instance, were seen as partial anticipations or "types" of Christ, so exemplary figures of pagan myth—notably Orpheus and Hercules, who had descended into hell and returned— could be made over, after a fashion, even if their virtue was a relatively pale shadow of more central and authentic types.

The whole tradition was thus summed up by George Chapman:

> . . . mysteries and allegorical fictions of Poesy . . . have . . .
> been of special reputation; . . . ever held in high reverence
> and authority, as supposed to conceal, within the outer bark
> (as their eternities approve), some sap of hidden truth, as
> either some dim and obscure prints of divinity and the sacred

---

[6]For Pandora and Eve see *Paradise Lost* iv. 714-720; for the long tradition, Dora and Erwin Panofsky, *Pandora's Box* (below, Bibliography, General).

[7]Much elevated and mystical allegorizing appeared, e.g., in the *Mythomystes* (1632) of the Platonist and minor poet, Henry Reynolds; see *Critical Essays of the Seventeenth Century*, ed. J. E. Spingarn (Oxford, 1908-1909), 1: pp. 141-179 (p. 175 for Noah-Noachus-Boachus-Bacchus). On Neoplatonic allegorizing of classical myth see Seznec and Edgar Wind, *Pagan Mysteries in the Renaissance* (New Haven, 1958). See also Don C. Allen's elaborate work, *The Legend of Noah: Renaissance Rationalism in Art, Science, and Letters* (Urbana, 1949), pp. 83-84, etc., and his *Doubt's Boundless Sea: Skepticism and Faith in the Renaissance* (Baltimore, 1964).

history, or the grounds of natural, or rules of moral, philosophy. . . .[8]

And, to add one more out of many witnesses, the same doctrine was affirmed by the Attendant Spirit in *Comus* (513-519). On the other hand, of course, in the sixteenth and seventeenth as in earlier centuries there was religious and moral condemnation of pagan myth, eventually from Milton himself; but this kind of hostility may be taken for granted.

Such traditional views of myth prepare us for ambivalent attitudes on the part of the more devoutly Christian poets, Milton in particular—although "ambivalent" is perhaps a misleading term for the conscious welcome of myths fully recognized as far outside saving Christian truth. The deeply religious and very eclectic Spenser manifests almost no trace of a scruple in blending the pagan and Christian. In his first volume, *The Shepherd's Calendar* (1579), Spenser in different pastoral allegories takes Pan to signify Christ, the Pope, and Henry VIII.[9] (Henry is not linked, as a sacrilegious modern might expect, with the goatish Pan; he is the father of the paragon of rural nymphs, Queen Elizabeth—who herself, in the poetical minds of her age, has the grand roles of Diana and Astraea.)[10] Behind the association of Pan with Christ were the myth of Pan as the god of shepherds and the image of Christ as the good shepherd. In Milton's first great English poem, *On the Morning of Christ's Nativity*, the shepherds near Bethlehem, "simply chatting" of their loves or their sheep, had no notion

> That the mighty Pan
> Was kindly come to live with them below.

There was too the etymological-metaphysical conception of Pan as "All," which naturally attached itself to Him by whom

---

[8]Quoted (in modernized form) from *The Poems of George Chapman*, ed. Phyllis B. Bartlett (New York, 1941), p. 327.

[9]Pan is Christ or God in *May* 54, 111, *July* 49, 144; the Pope in *July* 179; Henry VIII in *April* 51, 91.

[10]See Elkin C. Wilson, *England's Eliza* (Cambridge, Mass., 1939); Frances A. Yates, "Queen Elizabeth as Astraea," *JWCI* 10 (1947): pp. 27-82. *Cf.* Marjorie H. Nicolson, *The Breaking of the Circle* (rev. ed., New York, 1960), pp. 91 f.

all things were made, or, as in Ben Jonson's masque *Oberon,*
could be attached, with hyperbolical effort, to King James. In
Jonson's *Pan's Anniversary*

> Pan is our All, by him we breathe, we live,
> We move, we are.

This, as a critic remarks,[11] is a daring application of St. Paul's
saying: "For in him we live, and move, and have our being:
as certain also of your own poets have said, For we are also
his offspring" (Acts 17:28). In connection with the whole
pagan-Christian tradition we may note that St. Paul is here
avowedly quoting a pagan poet, Aratus.[12]

We must recall a haunting story told by Plutarch, without
Christian reference, in his treatise *The Obsolescence of Oracles,*
and by Bishop Eusebius, who took Pan as a demon. I quote,
with some abridgment, the different version included in
the original notes on the *May* eclogue in *The Shepherd's
Calendar:*[13]

> . . . about the same time, that our Lord suffered his most
> bitter passion for the redemption of man, certain passengers
> sailing from Italy to Cyprus and passing by certain isles called
> Paxae, heard a voice calling aloud "Thamus, Thamus" (now
> Thamus was . . . an Egyptian, . . . pilot of the ship), who,
> giving ear to the cry, was bidden, when he came to Palodes,

---

11John C. Meagher, *Method and Meaning in Jonson's Masques* (Notre Dame,
1966), pp. 45 and 192, n. 42; *Ben Jonson,* ed. C. H. Herford and P. and E. M.
Simpson (Oxford, 1925-1952), 7: pp. 353, 535.

12Aratus, *Phaenomena,* line 5. The phrase was cited by Milton in his mar-
ginalia on Aratus; he compared Lucretius, ii. 991-992 *(Works,* Columbia ed.,
18: p. 325; M. Kelley and S. D. Adkins, "Milton's Annotations of Aratus,"
PMLA 70 (1955) : p. 1092).

13Plutarch, *Obsolescence of Oracles (Moralia,* Loeb Classical Library, 5: pp.
401-403) ; Eusebius, *Preparation for the Gospel* 5. 17 (tr. E. H. Gifford, Oxford,
1903) 1: pp. 224-225. E. K.'s version in the *Shepherd's Calendar* is that of L.
Lavater, *Of ghostes and spirites walking by nyght* (tr., London, 1572; ed. J. D.
Wilson and M. Yardley, London, 1929, pp. 94-95 in both editions). The tradition, from Plutarch down, is surveyed by G. A. Gerhard ("Der Tod des
grossen Pan," *Sitzungsberichte der Heidelberger Akademie der Wissenschaften:
Philosophisch-historische Klasse* 5 (1915): pp. 3-52) and by Patricia Merivale
(below, Bibliography, General). Plutarch's story is closely examined by H.
Haakh, "Der grosse Pan ist tot" *(Das Altertum* 4 (1958) : pp. 105-110). See C.
A. Patrides, "The Cessation of the Oracles: The History of a Legend" *(MLR*
60 (1965): pp. 500-507), and M. Y. Hughes (n. 44 below).

to tell that the great Pan was dead: which he doubting to do, yet for that when he came to Palodes there suddenly was such a calm of wind that the ship stood still in the sea unmoved, he was forced to cry aloud that Pan was dead: wherewithal there was heard such piteous outcries and dreadful shrieking as hath not been the like. By which Pan, though of some be understood the great Satanas, whose kingdom at that time was by Christ conquered, the gates of hell broken up, and death by death delivered to eternal death (for at that time . . . all oracles surceased, and enchanted spirits, that were wont to delude the people, thenceforth held their peace), and also at the demand of the emperor Tiberius who that Pan should be, answer was made him by the wisest and best learned that it was the son of Mercury and Penelope, yet I think it more properly meant of the death of Christ, the only and very Pan, then suffering for his flock.

This story, traditionally associated with the Crucifixion, was probably in Milton's mind when he described the rout of the pagan gods at the birth of Christ:

> The lonely mountains o'er,
> And the resounding shore,
>   A voice of weeping heard, and loud lament;
> From haunted spring and dale,
> Edged with poplar pale,
>   The parting Genius is with sighing sent;
> With flow'r-inwoven tresses torn
> The nymphs in twilight shade of tangled thickets mourn.

The lines have a touch of nostalgia. The young Milton was fervently sincere in glorifying Christ and banishing the gods of idolatry; yet he was here, and always remained, responsive to the elements of beauty in the pagan myths. There is no more arresting example of the different attitudes possible to a single mind than the juxtaposition of the *Nativity* and the fifth of Milton's Latin elegies, written in the spring of the same year (1629). The elegy is a completely, though innocently, pagan poem, a likewise fervent celebration of the awakening of spring in the heavens, on the earth, in young men and women, and in the gods who come down to sport in field and wood. The poem is packed with mythological and sexual images (including the lustful Pan), and it ends with a prayer that the gods may not forsake the groves of earth—the gods whose overthrow the young poet was soon to exult in. But Christian fervor does not necessarily extinguish all the feelings of the natural man.

Milton continually blends and differentiates Christian and pagan. In *Lycidas*, facing the grim fact of premature death and God's apparent injustice, he abandons the conventional vain questioning of the nymphs who might have been present to save and recalls the fate of the archetypal poet in the most harshly resonant lines he had yet written:[14]

> What could the Muse herself that Orpheus bore,
> The Muse herself, for her enchanting son
> Whom universal nature did lament,
> When by the rout that made the hideous roar
> His gory visage down the stream was sent,
> Down the swift Hebrus to the Lesbian shore?

The first answer to that is the seeming futility of virtue, study, and talent in a world where such things can happen. But the death that appears to be the work of a "blind Fury" must be seen through the eyes of "all-judging Jove." The final vision of the dead man's reception into heaven sweeps away all questioning of God's justice and love, and the poem returns, in pastoral vein, to earthly life: the spirit of Lycidas will be a Christian "Genius of the shore," an agent of "the dear might of him that walked the waves."

A vignette similar in ambivalence to the stanza quoted from the *Nativity* is the picture of the fall of Mulciber in the first book of *Paradise Lost* (740-747). Using the patristic tradition that the fallen angels became the heathen gods, Milton had just given an epic roll-call which is a vehement survey of the later spread of idolatry, but for a moment the pure artist takes command and transforms Homer's half-comic account of Hephaestus' fall into romantic beauty:

> . . . and how he fell
> From heav'n, they fabled, thrown by angry Jove

14See Caroline W. Mayerson, "The Orpheus Image in *Lycidas*," *PMLA* **64** (1949): pp. 189-207; and essays collected in *Lycidas: The Tradition and the Poem*, ed. C. A. Patrides (New York, 1961).

> Sheer o'er the crystal battlements: from morn
> To noon he fell, from noon to dewy eve,
> A summer's day; and with the setting sun
> Dropped from the zenith like a falling star,
> On Lemnos th'Aegean isle. Thus they relate,
> Erring . . . .

Here the changes of pace and of vowels suggest smooth float-
ing, then swifter motion coming suddenly to rest, all with an
un-Homeric sense of vast space and of the uncontaminated
beauty of nature—and yet, as in some other places, the
momentary vision is framed in explicit assertions of its falsity.[15]
Nothing shows more clearly the invincible potency of Milton's
classical instincts than one image in that poem of austere
passion, *Paradise Regained.* In a climactic speech, a speech
that has unduly disturbed many readers, Christ condemns most
Greek culture, including its religious mythology, and, speaking
of the pride and ignorance of pagan philosophies, declares:

> Who therefore seeks in these
> True wisdom, finds her not, or by delusion
> Far worse, her false resemblance only meets,
> An empty cloud.

The image comes from the myth of Ixion, who, presump-
tuously trying to embrace the goddess Hera, embraced a cloud
instead and thereby begot the misshapen Centaurs.

In English poetry of the Renaissance mythology, whether
or not it was given a religious connection, was strongly ethical.
The two chief translators of Ovid's *Metamorphoses* exemplified
and fortified the tradition. In 1567 Arthur Golding, in his
lengthy prefaces in verse, expounded the moral lessons for young
and old to be found in Ovid's tales. The much more sophisti-

---

[15]The young Milton had a brief but similarly serious—and wholly sympathetic—allusion to Hephaestus' fall in his Latin *Elegy* 7. 81-82. For
Milton's expressions of religious skepticism or scruple about classical myth see
the early *On the Death of a Fair Infant* (line 40) and *Paradise Lost* i. 197,
446-452, 477-482, 507-510, 740-747, ii. 627-628, iv. 250-251, 706, v. 381, vii. 1-7,
39, ix. 439-443, x. 578-584, xi. 10-14, *Paradise Regained* ii. 178-191, 214-215,
357-358, iv. 339-342, 563-564, *Samson Agonistes* 150, 499-501 (these last two
items are a matter of Hebraic decorum). Of course Milton makes many mythological allusions without comment.

cated George Sandys—whose translation, published complete in 1626, was the first literary work in English done in America —in 1632 added a full commentary, with a much wider allegorical range than Golding's, based on interpreters from Plato up to Bacon. In this context the name of Bacon may be a surprising reminder of the strength of the tradition: we might not have expected the prophet of the new science to write a book of allegorized myths—though Bacon was slightly apologetic and though his interpretations were mainly scientific and political.[16] Three notably humanistic poets are more central witnesses, all of them indebted to Renaissance handbooks as well as to ancient literature. Spenser, one of the supreme mythmakers in English poetry, made continual and richly decorative use of mythological image and symbol in developing ethical and religious themes in the *Faerie Queene* and elsewhere; in the incomparable *Epithalamion* pagan myth contributes to the celebration of love and marriage as a citadel or shrine of Christian order and beauty in a menacing world.[17] Ben Jonson, the great master of court masques, invested spectacular and musical entertainments with serious moral allegory and sym-

---

[16]C. W. Lemmi, *The Classic Deities in Bacon: A Study in Mythological Symbolism* (Baltimore, 1933); Elizabeth Sewell, *The Orphic Voice: Poetry and Natural History* (New Haven, 1960).

[17]For Spenser's use of classical myth some references are: H. G. Lotspeich, *Classical Mythology in the Poetry of Edmund Spenser* (Princeton, 1932); C. W. Lemmi, "The Symbolism of the Classical Episodes in *The Faerie Queene*," *Philological Quarterly* 8 (1929): pp. 270-287, on the moralizations of the mythographer Natalis Comes; the commentaries in the Variorum Edition of Spenser; M. Y. Hughes, "Virgilian Allegory and *The Faerie Queene*," *PMLA* 44 (1929): pp. 696-705, and n. 22 below; Bush and Starnes and Talbert (Bibliography, I, below); A. C. Hamilton, "Spenser's Treatment of Myth," *ELH* 26 (1959): pp. 335-354, and *The Structure of Allegory in The Faerie Queene* (Oxford, 1961); N. Frye, "The Structure of Imagery in *The Faerie Queene*," *UTQ* 30 (1960-1961): pp. 109-127, repr. in *Fables of Identity* (New York, 1963); Kathleen Williams, "Venus and Diana: Some Uses of Myth in *The Faerie Queene*," *ELH* 28 (1961): pp. 101-120, and *Spenser's World of Glass* (Berkeley, 1966); *Books I and II of The Faerie Queene, the Mutability Cantos, and Selections from The Minor Poetry*, ed. R. Kellogg and O. Steele (New York, 1965), *passim*; and books and articles cited below, in nn. 23, 24, 45, 46, 48. F. Kermode ("Spenser and the Allegorists," *Proceedings of the British Academy* 48 (1962)) deals chiefly with the Biblical, political, and generally broad senses of Spenser's "myths."

bolism[18]—for instance, in the masque often cited in connection with *Comus, Pleasure Reconciled to Virtue*, where Hercules is the exemplar of active virtue. George Chapman, in his translations of Homer, could use Platonic and Stoic language to bring out the ethical implications he saw in the divine poet;[19] and it has been observed that the chief figures in Chapman's tragedies tend to resemble one or other of Homer's protagonists, Achilles, the passionate man of action, or Odysseus, the man of overruling wisdom and endurance.[20] In his original poems, such as his continuation of Marlowe's *Hero and Leander*, Chapman can expound his humanistic and Christian doctrine of order through very complex mythological symbolism.[21]

---

[18]On the mythological and ethical symbolism of Jonson's masques see articles by D. J. Gordon in *JWCI* 6 (1943): pp. 122-141 and 8 (1945): pp. 107-145 and *MLR* 42 (1947): pp. 180-187; Allan H. Gilbert, *The Symbolic Persons in the Masques of Ben Jonson* (Durham, N. C., 1948); Starnes and Talbert (Bibliography, I, below); Stephen Orgel, *The Jonsonian Masque* (Cambridge, Mass., 1965); J. C. Meagher (n. 11 above). Charles F. Wheeler *(Classical Mythology in the Plays, Masques, and Poems of Ben Jonson* (Princeton, 1938)) gives a full catalogue of the data and of ancient authorities but neglects Renaissance writers.

[19]In addition to F. L. Schoell's basic *Études sur l'humanisme continental en Angleterre* (Paris, 1926), some studies are: D. Smalley, "The Ethical Bias of Chapman's Homer," *SP* 36 (1939): pp. 169-191; P. B. Bartlett, "The Heroes of Chapman's Homer," *RES* 17 (1941): pp. 257-280; W. Schrickx, "George Chapman's Borrowings from Natali Conti," *English Studies* 32 (1951): pp. 107-112, a supplement to Schoell; G. deF. Lord, *Homeric Renaissance: The Odyssey of George Chapman* (New Haven, 1956); R. Sühnel, *Homer und die englische Humanität* (Tübingen, 1958); E. Phinney, "Continental Humanists and Chapman's *Iliads*," *Studies in the Renaissance* 12 (1965): pp. 218-226. The latest general studies are Millar MacLure's *George Chapman* (Toronto, 1966) and Charlotte Spivack's *George Chapman* (New York, 1967).

[20]Ennis Rees, *The Tragedies of George Chapman* (Cambridge, Mass., 1954), pp. 29 f. Rees' first chapter is an excellent account of "Chapman's Christian Humanism." *Cf.* E. Schwartz *(JEGP* 56 (1957): pp. 163-176), E. M. Waith (Bibliography, I, below), M. MacLure (n. 19 above), and R. B. Waddington (n. 21 below).

[21]D. J. Gordon, "Chapman's 'Hero and Leander,' " *English Miscellany* 5 (Rome, 1954): pp. 41-94. Along with the books on Chapman (nn. 19 and 20 above), two general essays are: C. S. Lewis, "Hero and Leander," *Proceedings of the British Academy* 38 (1952): pp. 23-37, repr. in *Elizabethan Poetry: Modern Essays in Criticism*, ed. P. J. Alpers (New York, 1967); and V. Kostič, "Marlowe's *Hero and Leander* and Chapman's Continuation," *Renaissance and Modern Essays Presented to V. de Sola Pinto*, ed. G. R. Hibbard (London, 1966), pp. 25-34.

For two other works, see R. B. Waddington, "Chapman's *Andromeda Liberata*: Mythology and Meaning," *PMLA* 81 (1966): pp. 34-44, and "Prometheus and Hercules: The Dialectic of *Bussy D'Ambois*," *ELH* 34 (1967): pp. 21-48.

The moralized myth perhaps most typical of the Renaissance was the story of Circe.[22] In Ariosto, Tasso, Spenser, and lesser poets, and, with variations, in *Comus*, the theme is heroic man's confronting sensual temptation which threatens his integrity and enterprise; it had been so understood by Horace (*Epistles* I.ii.17-31) and perhaps by Homer himself. Among such treatments those of Spenser and Milton are, in partly different ways, the most elaborate and subtle. Spenser's Guyon, the knight of temperance, and his attendant Palmer, representative of reason, encounter a succession of perils and allurements on their way to the Bower of Bliss and its sensual mistress, Acrasia. Spenser describes every kind of beauty associated with traditional earthly paradises, but the subtlety of his picture-making and seductive rhythms is in the continual suggestion both of nature's purity tainted by artificial excess and of sterile titillation of the senses in contrast with healthy fruition. The older romantic criticism of Spenser saw in the destruction of the Bower a Puritan hostility to beauty—as if Guyon should or could have transformed a nursery of corruption by putting up a sign, "Reopened under new management." Modern critics have had more discriminating insight.[23] The earlier temptations offered Guyon by Mammon in his underworld are modeled on Satan's temptation of Christ in the wilderness

---

22See M. Y. Hughes, "Spenser's Acrasia and the Circe of the Renaissance," *Journal of the History of Ideas* 4 (1943): pp. 381-399; R. M. Durling, "The Bower of Bliss and Armida's Palace," *CL* 6 (1954): pp. 335-347; A. B. Giamatti (n. 5 above), on Ariosto, Tasso, Spenser, *et al.*, with copious references.

23Romantic misinterpretation was rectified by C. S. Lewis, *The Allegory of Love* (Oxford, 1938), pp. 324-333. Lewis' analysis has in turn been modified and refined by N. S. Brooks, "C. S. Lewis and Spenser: Nature, Art and the Bower of Bliss," *Cambridge Journal* 2 (1948-1949): pp. 420-434; H. Berger, *The Allegorical Temper: Vision and Reality in Book II of Spenser's Faerie Queene* (New Haven, 1957), pp. 211-240; H. P. Guth, "Allegorical Implications of Artifice in Spenser's *Faerie Queene*," *PMLA* 76 (1961): pp. 474-479; M. MacLure, "Nature and Art in *The Faerie Queene*," *ELH* 28 (1961): pp. 1-20; Ruth Nevo, "Spenser's 'Bower of Bliss' and a Key Metaphor from Renaissance Poetic," *Studies in Western Literature*, ed. D. A. Fineman (Jerusalem, Oxford, 1962), pp. 20-31; A. B. Giamatti (n. 5 above); K. Williams and Kellogg and Steele (n. 17 above); Paul J. Alpers, *The Poetry of The Faerie Queene* (Princeton, 1967).

Two broad treatments of Renaissance conceptions of nature are: Edward W. Tayler, *Nature and Art in Renaissance Literature* (New York, 1964), and Eric LaGuardia, *Nature Redeemed* (The Hague, 1966). *Cf.* D. Cheney (n. 46 below).

and the medieval tradition of Christ's harrowing of hell; the two particularized sinners whom Guyon sees are Tantalus and Pontius Pilate (II.vii.57-62). This is the only book of the *Faerie Queene* in which an angel appears (to protect the exhausted and unconscious Guyon), and Maleger (II.xi), the enemy of soul and body, seems to be original sin, for which there is no remedy except the water of baptism.[24]

As Spenser gives a religious dimension to his account of the classical, rational virtue of temperance, so in *Comus*, where the protagonist is the Lady and the sorcerer-seducer is Circe's son, Milton unites reason and religion, though Christian reference is thinly veiled until the end. The children's journey through the dark wood to Ludlow typifies man's earthly life, and the Attendant Spirit has the function of a guardian angel. The philosophic Elder Brother expounds rational virtue. The wicked enchanter, in his debate with the Lady, utters poetry of uniquely tactual and visual power; he argues that Nature's bounties are for use and goes on to the conventional libertine plea for sensual license. The Lady's reply is at first a rational defense of temperance, but she rises with "sacred vehemence" to a religious view beyond Comus' grasp. The magical plant, haemony, is the Miltonic equivalent of the Homeric moly, which protected Odysseus against Circe and which had long been allegorized as

---

[24] Book II of the *Faerie Queene* is of course treated in the general studies of Spenser or the poem, e.g., M. Pauline Parker, *The Allegory of the Faerie Queene* (Oxford, 1960), pp. 114-162; A. C. Hamilton (n. 17 above); Graham Hough, *A Preface to The Faerie Queene* (New York, 1963), pp. 154-166; W. Nelson (n. 46 below), pp. 178-203; A. B. Giamatti (n. 5 above), pp. 247-283; and the edition of Kellogg and Steele (n. 17 above). Some special interpretations are: A. S. P. Woodhouse, "Nature and Grace in *The Faerie Queene*," *ELH* 16 (1949): pp. 194-228, repr. in J. R. Kreuzer and L. Cogan, *Modern Writings on Major English Authors* (Indianapolis, 1963); Robert Hoopes, "'God Guide Thee, Guyon': Nature and Grace Reconciled in *The Faerie Queene*, Book II," *RES* 5 (1954): pp. 14-24; H. Berger (n. 23 above); B. Nellish, "The Allegory of Guyon's Voyage: An Interpretation," *ELH* 30 (1963): pp. 89-106; P. J. Alpers (n. 23 above), pp. 235-278, on the episode of Mammon. Woodhouse's interpretation of Maleger as original sin seems to have been generally accepted; it is opposed by L. H. Miller, "Arthur, Maleger, and History," *UTQ* 35 (1965-1966): pp. 176-187. Miller also opposes current orthodoxy in "A Secular Reading of *The Faerie Queene*, Book II," *ELH* 33 (1966): pp. 154-169.

temperance.[25] When the brothers rush in and Comus escapes,
the Lady can be freed from his spell only by Sabrina, the goddess of the Severn river, who seems to represent divine grace.[26]
The epilogue becomes overtly Christian: the youth and freedom and joy that Comus claims for himself belong really and
only to virtue, which leads to heaven. The final couplet is at
once a religious statement and a poetic incantation:

> Or, if Virtue feeble were,
> Heav'n itself would stoop to her.

The basic appeal that mythological figures held for Renaissance poets, Christian or secular, was their ideal quality—ideal
sometimes morally, but often in the non-moral sense of power,
beauty, passion, beyond human limits. Imaginative response to
such beings was fuller and easier then than it has usually been
since because everyone grew up on the classics, because the
visible and invisible world was still a network of related symbols, because the classical figures readily mixed with the
familiar spirits of native folklore (as in Prospero's speech to
the "elves of hills, brooks, standing lakes, and groves," or in
the long "Digression of the Nature of Spirits" in Burton's

25For the traditional allegorization of the Homeric moly see Robert M.
Adams, *Ikon: Milton and the Modern Critics* (Ithaca, 1955), p. 14, n. 5; Hugo
Rahner (Bibliography, General, below), pp. 179-222. George Sandys' allegorical
interpretation of Circe and Odysseus is partly quoted in D. Bush, *Renaissance
Tradition* (ed. 1932), pp. 267-268; (ed. 1963), p. 280.
The many modern discussions of *Comus* will be summarized in the Variorum
Commentary on Milton's poetry which is being prepared by M. Y. Hughes and
others. A few of these are: A. S. P. Woodhouse, "The Argument of Milton's
Comus," *UTQ* 11 (1941-1942): pp. 46-71, and "*Comus* Once More," *ibid.* 19
(1949-1950): pp. 218-223, the latter on Sabrina; J. Arthos, *On A Mask Pre-
sented at Ludlow-Castle* (Ann Arbor, 1954); R. M. Adams, *Ikon* (above), pp.
1-34; R. Tuve, *Images & Themes in Five Poems by Milton* (Cambridge, Mass.,
1957), pp. 112-161; W. G. Madsen, "The Idea of Nature in Milton's Poetry,"
Three Studies in the Renaissance, by Richard B. Young, W. T. Furniss, and
W. G. Madsen (New Haven, 1958), pp. 185-218; C. L. Barber, "*A Mask Presented at Ludlow Castle*: The Masque as a Masque," *The Lyric and Dramatic
Milton*, ed. Joseph H. Summers (New York, 1965); E. LaGuardia (n. 23 above);
and B. Rajan, "Comus: *The Inglorious Likeness*," *UTQ* 37 (1967-1968): pp.
113-135. A number of essays on *Comus* are collected in *A Maske at Ludlow*,
ed. John S. Diekhoff (Cleveland, 1968). J. G. Demaray's *Milton and the
Masque Tradition* (Cambridge, Mass., 1968) is concerned mainly with formal
elements.
26Woodhouse, "*Comus* Once More" (n. 25 above).

Anatomy of Melancholy), and because Christian belief had filled earth and sky with supernatural beings, good and bad. The gods and demigods of classical myth were, so to speak, naturalistic counterparts of the angels and were far more substantial, individual, and usable.

Before proceeding with mythology in religious and moral contexts we must take more account of the naturalistic secular strain, and we may look first, and briefly, at the extreme end of the spectrum. One way of evading, if not often transcending, the normal limits or conventions of life is represented by a kind of poem which was cultivated all over Europe. This was a narrative of some length, recounting usually one Ovidian myth, but in a lavish and luscious Italianate manner that went far beyond the fairly pictorial Ovid and emulated Renaissance painting and tapestry.[27] Of the many English pieces the best-known are of course Marlowe's *Hero and Leander* and Shakespeare's *Venus and Adonis*. While the former is not mythological, its allusions are part of Marlowe's exuberant response to beauty, passion, and energy; and the poem had a strong influence on the mythological narratives that followed.[28] *Venus*

[27]A dozen of these poems (with Chapman's translation of the Greek poem on Hero and Leander) have been edited by Elizabeth S. Donno as *Elizabethan Minor Epics* (London, 1963). The best-known authors included are Lodge, Marlowe, Chapman, Heywood, Drayton, Marston, Francis Beaumont (?), P. Fletcher, Shirley. Several Ovidian tales are included in *Seven Minor Epics of the English Renaissance (1596-1624)*, ed. Paul W. Miller (Gainesville, 1967), and half a dozen classical or mythological poems in *Elizabethan Narrative Verse*, ed. N. Alexander (London and Cambridge, Mass., 1968). These and other poems of the kind are more or less discussed by D. Bush, M. C. Bradbrook, and H. Smith (Bibliography, I, below), by L. R. Zocca, *Elizabethan Narrative Poetry* (New Brunswick, 1950), P. W. Miller, *SP* 55 (1958): pp. 31-38, C. Leech, *SEL* 5 (1965): pp. 247-268, and the several recent editors. For *Hero and Leander* and *Venus and Adonis* see the next two notes.

[28]*Hero and Leander* is annotated in *Marlowe's Poems*, ed. L. C. Martin (London and New York, 1931). It is discussed by L. Chabalier, *Héro et Léandre* (Paris, 1911), in the books by D. Bush, M. C. Bradbrook, H. Smith (Bibliography, I, below), and, from her special point of view, in Rosemond Tuve's *Elizabethan and Metaphysical Imagery* (Chicago, 1947), pp. 251-280; and in the books on Marlowe by J. Bakeless (1942), M. Poirier (1951), H. Levin (1952), and J. B. Steane (Cambridge, 1964). Some essays are: P. W. Miller, *SP* 50 (1953): pp. 158-167; R. Fraser, *JEGP* 57 (1958): pp. 743-754; E. B. Cantelupe, *College English* 24 (1962-1963): pp. 295-298; C. Leech (n. 27 above); E. Segal, "Hero and Leander: Góngora and Marlowe," *CL* 15 (1963): pp. 338-356. Echoes of *Hero and Leander* in subsequent mythological poems were recorded by D. Bush, *MLN* 42 (1927): pp 211-217; Bakeless (above), 2: pp. 114-148.

and Adonis is a tissue of ultra-Ovidian rhetoric in which the two personages are pretty well demythologized. Some modern critics have discerned various philosophic themes in it, and others comedy; Elizabethan readers seem to have relished chiefly the decorative eroticism that was the staple of the genre.[29] Even the young clergyman, Phineas Fletcher, produced a decidedly unclerical poem, *Venus and Anchises*. One notable exception was Drayton's Platonic *Endimion and Phoebe*, in which Phoebe (Diana) initiates her shepherd lover into celestial knowledge; the plot of this poem anticipated that of Keats's *Endymion*. Another exception was Chapman's *Ovid's Banquet of Sense*, which, though not mythological, was related, in darkly "Platonic" hostility, to the Ovidian type. In a number of these tales the erotic temperature was more or less lowered by humor and mocking wit. Apart from a few poems, this minor genre is of interest mainly in its outflanking of the central ethical tradition. At the same time such pieces had their own kind of idealism, an uninhibited and usually unmoralized sense of beauty in nature, art, and the human body, so that they are not wholly divorced from the poetry of Spenser and others in which sensuous or sensual beauty serves a moral end.

29*Venus and Adonis* is discussed in the New Variorum edition of Shakespeare's *Poems*, ed. H. E. Rollins (Philadelphia, 1938), the new Arden edition of F. T. Prince (1960), the Cambridge edition of J. C. Maxwell (1966). Recent interpretations are surveyed by J. W. Lever, *Shakespeare Survey* 15 (1962): pp. 18-21, and K. Muir, *"Venus and Adonis:* Comedy or Tragedy?" *Shakespearean Essays*, ed. Alwin Thaler and N. Sanders (Knoxville, 1964). Some studies are: H. T. Price, "Function of Imagery in *Venus and Adonis,*" *Papers of the Michigan Academy* 31 (1945): pp. 275-297; T. W. Baldwin, *On the Literary Genetics of Shakspere's Poems & Sonnets* (Urbana, 1950); W. B. C. Watkins, *Shakespeare and Spenser* (Princeton, 1950), pp. 5-27; R. Putney, "Venus Agonistes," *University of Colorado Studies* 4 (1953): pp. 52-66; F. M. Dickey, *Not Wisely But Too Well: Shakespeare's Love Tragedies* (San Marino, 1957), chap. 5; R. S. Jackson, "Narrative and Imagery in Shakespeare's *Venus and Adonis,*" *Papers of the Michigan Academy* 43 (1958): pp. 315-320; D. C. Allen, "On *Venus and Adonis,*" *Elizabethan and Jacobean Studies* (1959: cited below in n. 36); A. C. Hamilton, *SEL* 1 (1961): pp. 1-15; articles by M. C. Bradbrook, A. Bonjour, and J. W. Lever, *Shakespeare Survey* 15 (1962); D. Bush, *Renaissance Tradition*, pp. 137-148; E. B. Cantelupe, *Shakespeare Quarterly* 14 (1963); C. Butler and A. Fowler, in *Shakespeare 1564-1964,* ed. E. A. Bloom (Providence, 1964), another exposition of numerology; C. Leech (n. 27 above); Norman Rabkin, in *Pacific Coast Studies in Shakespeare,* ed. W. F. McNeir and T. N. Greenfield (Eugene, (1966), pp. 20-32), and Rabkin's *Shakespeare and the Common Understanding* (New York, 1967) pp. 150-162.

Mythological figures as symbols of superhuman capacities or natural forces are everywhere in Renaissance literature and we can only note a few diverse examples and different degrees of poetic value. On the lowest level we find mere grammar-school learning, flat mythological data rhetorically inflated. This sort of thing, natural enough in its age, we may disregard —though it is frequent in Shakespeare, especially in his early plays, and may appear in his latest, as when Prospero, in the speech already cited, addresses the elves who "chase the ebbing Neptune." On higher levels allusion is at least functional, and often inspired. Thus Prince Hal, the supposed playboy, is described to the contemptuous Hotspur as mounting his horse

> like feathered Mercury,
> . . . .
>
> As if an angel dropp'd down from the clouds
> To turn and wind a fiery Pegasus . . . .[30]

We may observe the casual mixture of the classical and Christian. Hamlet in soliloquy contrasts his father and his uncle as "Hyperion to a satyr"; and, upbraiding his mother with the same contrast, he invokes Hyperion, Jove, Mars, and Mercury.

Even the mortal figures of myth and story may become glamorous emblems of human mortality or promise the fulfillment of immortal longings. One need not apologize for citing the most familiar examples, the first two from Thomas Nashe and Marlowe:

> Brightness falls from the air,
> Queens have died young and fair,
> Dust hath closed Helen's eye.
> I am sick, I must die.
> Lord, have mercy on us!

---

[30] *1 Henry IV* IV. i. 106 f. The postclassical substitution of Perseus for Bellerophon as the rider of Pegasus is traced by T. W. Baldwin, "Perseus Purloins Pegasus," *Philological Quarterly* 20 (1941): pp. 361-370. See also Mary Lascelles, "The Rider on the Winged Horse," *Elizabethan and Jacobean Studies* (n. 36 below), pp. 173-198; J. M. Steadman, "'Perseus upon Pegasus' and *Ovid Moralized*," *RES* 9 (1958): pp. 407-410.

> Was this the face that launched a thousand ships,
> And burnt the topless towers of Ilium?
> Sweet Helen, make me immortal with a kiss.

Faustus, we remember, is deluded as well as damned.[31] At the end of *The Merchant of Venice* the happy Lorenzo and Jessica, in their lyrical moonlight dialogue, recall famous and unfortunate lovers, among them Dido, an un-Virgilian Dido drawn from Chaucer's picture of the deserted Ariadne:[32]

> In such a night
> Stood Dido with a willow in her hand
> Upon the wild sea-banks, and waft her love
> To come again to Carthage.

No less romantic, but inspired by the false report of Cleopatra's death and his own resolve on suicide, is Antony's vision of renewed life and love (IV.xiv.50-54):

> I come, my queen. . . . Stay for me.
> Where souls do couch on flowers, we'll hand in hand
> And with our sprightly port make the ghosts gaze.
> Dido and her Aeneas shall want troops,
> And all the haunt be ours.

Allusions may build a remote, unearthly world of the imagination, or they may lift everyday things into ideal perfection. In *The Winter's Tale* (IV.iv.116-122) the fresh, sensuous actuality of the English spring is given a mythic heightening:

> O Proserpina,
> For the flowers now that, frighted, thou let'st fall
> From Dis's wagon! daffodils,
> That come before the swallow dares and take
> The winds of March with beauty; violets—dim,
> But sweeter than the lids of Juno's eyes
> Or Cytherea's breath. . . .

---

[31]See T. McAlindon, "Classical Mythology and Christian Tradition in Marlowe's *Doctor Faustus*," *PMLA* 81 (1966): pp. 214-223.

[32]R. K. Root (n. 36 below), p. 57; Chaucer, *The Legend of Good Women* vi, "Ariadne," lines 2185-2206.

Andrew Marvell, celebrating the green contemplative solitude
of a garden, can transpose Ovid's erotic myths into swift images
of artistic creation:

> The gods, that mortal beauty chase,
> Still in a tree did end their race.
> Apollo hunted Daphne so,
> Only that she might laurel grow.
> And Pan did after Syrinx speed,
> Not as a nymph, but for a reed.

In these and countless other passages, abstract phrases could
not achieve the effect of names that carry such a supramundane
aura. So used, mythology becomes a kind of evocative short-
hand, a language that satisfies the human need for imaginative and emotional transcendence of mortal and earthly
imperfection.

The good and the bad figures of mythology were likely to
remain good or bad in Christian tradition, but some, as we
have partly seen, might acquire new associations and meanings.
Professor Waith has shown at large the presence of, to quote
the title of his book, *The Herculean Hero in Marlowe, Chapman, Shakespeare, and Dryden* (1962).[33] We have already
noticed the virtuous Hercules in Jonson's masque. Hamlet, in
self-disparagement, more than once thinks of the active Hercules (I.ii.153, I.iv.83, V.i.314). In Shakespeare's picture of
Antony's fall from greatness to ruin a minute item is altered
from Plutarch, the allusion to strange music that betokens
Antony's being abandoned by Bacchus; in the play (IV.iii.15-16)

> 'Tis the god Hercules, whom Antony lov'd,
> Now leaves him—

the Hercules from whom Antony traced his descent, and whose
rage, a little later (IV.xii.43 f.), he would emulate. The same

---

[33]In addition to Waith see, e.g., Rolf Soellner, "The Madness of Hercules
and the Elizabethans," *CL* **10** (1958) : pp. 309-324. *Cf.* R. B. Waddington (n.
21 above); Jean MacIntyre, "Spenser's Herculean Heroes," *Humanities Association Bulletin* (Canada) **17** (1966) : pp. 5-12; n. 34 below; and R. Knowles
(n. 36 below).

incident, of Hercules' agonized death from the poisoned shirt, was used in very different contexts by Spenser and Milton: by Spenser to suggest the pains of St. George in his combat with the dragon (Satan) that is his crowning trial (*Faerie Queene* I.xi.27), by Milton to suggest the futile rage and violence of the fallen angels in hell (*Paradise Lost* ii.542 f.). Spenser's allusion was in accord with the allegorical tradition of the Hercules who toiled and suffered for others: as Alexander Ross said in his allegorical handbook of 1647, *Mystagogus Poeticus*: "Our blessed Saviour is the true Hercules." And at the end of Milton's *Nativity* the irresistible power of the infant Christ over the false gods prompts a veiled reference to the infant Hercules' strangling of the serpents.[34] In that poem's unfinished sequel, *The Passion,* Christ is tacitly likened to Hercules as a

> Most perfect Hero, tried in heaviest plight
> Of labors huge and hard, too hard for human wight.

To jump up forty years to *Paradise Regained,* when Satan has offered his last desperate challenge to Christ to stand on the pinnacle of the temple and himself falls while Christ stands, Milton (departing from the manner of the poem) brings in two classical similes, one of them about Hercules' defeat of the Earth-born giant Antaeus—a myth already used by Spenser for Arthur's victory over original sin.[35]

Our glances at Shakespeare have shown that his mythological allusions commonly partook of the common idealizing habit, the

---

[34]*Nativity,* lines 227-228. *Cf.* Alexander Ross, *Mystagogus Poeticus* (ed. 1648), p. 169. By far the most elaborate allegorical exposition was that of the chancellor of Florence, Coluccio Salutati, *De Laboribus Herculis,* ed. B. L. Ullman (2 v., Zurich, 1951). For one poetical example of the tradition, Ronsard's *Hercule Chrestien,* see Frances A. Yates, *The French Academies of the Sixteenth Century* (London, 1947), pp. 191-192. Marcel Simon's *Hercule et le Christianisme* (Paris, 1955) deals mainly with the early Christian centuries. *Cf.* Marc-René Jung (Bibliography, I, below).

[35]*Paradise Regained* iv. 562-568; *Faerie Queene* II. xi. 45-46. See K. Widmer, "The Iconography of Renunciation: The Miltonic Simile," *ELH* 25 (1958): pp. 258-259; H. Spevack-Husmann (n. 44 below), p. 139, etc.

raising of human figures—or even flowers—beyond actuality.[36] His references are mostly incidental and isolated, but something like a pattern of significance is suggested by the repeated linking of Hercules with Hamlet and Antony. Conscious design also seems to explain, in the opening of *King Lear*, the old king's angry appeals to the pagan gods, which initiate the continuing question of divine providence and justice.[37] Shakespeare, like Chaucer,[38] was normally a too instinctive realist to be drawn to the allegorical use of myth, but he approached that tradition in his latest group of plays. These tragicomedies or dramatic romances, full of theatrical if undramatic surprises, have seemed to depict evil overcome by good and, unlike the earlier tragedies, to reflect a relatively serene acceptance of life's mysteries.[39] The eventual power of good is symbolized in agents or acts of some sort of Providence; the most impressive of course is Prospero. But in most of these plays the symbolic agents of miraculous beneficence or redemption are classical deities. In *Pericles* there is repeated reference to Diana, goddess

[36]Comment on Shakespeare's dramatic use of classical myth appears *passim* in the annotated editions and many critical studies. The material was mapped out by Robert K. Root, *Classical Mythology in Shakespeare* (New York, 1903). See T. W. Baldwin, Starnes and Talbert, and J. A. K. Thomson in the Bibliography, I, below. Two short surveys by D. Bush are in *Elizabethan and Jacobean Studies Presented to Frank Percy Wilson*, ed. H. Davis and H. Gardner (Oxford, 1959), pp. 65-85, and *The Reader's Encyclopedia of Shakespeare*, ed. O. J. Campbell and E. G. Quinn (New York, 1966), pp. 116-119. A special Trojan item is H. Levin's "Explication of the Player's Speech" *(Kenyon Review* **12** (1950): pp. 273-296; *The Question of Hamlet* (New York, 1959)). The more or less veiled use of myth in Shakespeare—as in Spenser and Milton—is too complex to go into, but, for three recent and random illustrations, see A. R. McGee, " 'Macbeth' and the Furies," *Shakespeare Survey* **19** (1966): pp. 55-67; W. M. Merchant, " 'His Fiend-like Queen,' " *ibid.* pp. 75-81; I.-S. Ewbank, "The Fiend-like Queen: A Note on 'Macbeth' and Seneca's 'Medea,' " *ibid.* pp. 82-94. See also M. Andrews, "Lear's Wheel of Fire and Centaur Daughters," *Renaissance Papers 1965* (1966), pp. 21-24. Larger mythological dimensions in two plays are seen by Don C. Allen, *"The Tempest," Image and Meaning* (Baltimore, 1960), and Richard Knowles, "Myth and Type in *As You Like It*," *ELH* **33** (1966): pp. 1-22.

[37]William R. Elton, *King Lear and the Gods* (San Marino, 1966).

[38]One may still hold this traditional view of Chaucer, although some recent interpreters are busily turning him into an allegorical preacher.

[39]See the new Arden editions of the plays mentioned, and two surveys of critical interpretations: P. Edwards, "Shakespeare's Romances: 1900-1957," *Shakespeare Survey* **11** (1958): pp. 1-18: F. Kermode, *Shakespeare: The Final Plays* (British Council pamphlet, London, 1963); *Later Shakespeare*, ed. John R. Brown and B. Harris (Stratford-upon-Avon Studies 8, London, 1966).

of chastity, and Diana herself appears in vision as a *dea ex machina* (V.i). In a vision near the end of *Cymbeline* (V.iv) Jupiter descends to ordain a happy ending. In *The Winter's Tale* (III.ii) the unseen Apollo turns evil to good.[40] In *The Tempest* (IV.i) the goddesses Iris, Ceres, and Juno bless the betrothal of Ferdinand and Miranda. However, these mythological powers, perhaps inevitably in view of their function, have nothing of the vitality of many of Shakespeare's incidental allusions; they exist only in the total patterns of meaning—patterns which some modern critics have carried very far in the Christian direction.[41]

We may observe the fortunes of two very different figures of myth. One who, like Hercules, commonly remained pagan but had also been absorbed into Christian typology, was Orpheus, the musician whose lyre could move stones and trees, the devoted husband who went to hell and won back his dead wife, only to lose her again. Orpheus has filled the most diverse roles, from that of maker of the Orphic Hymns and founder of religious mysteries to that of hero in a medieval fairy romance, *Sir Orfeo*.[42] George Sandys, in his Ovidian com-

---

40Northrop Frye, "Recognition in *The Winter's Tale,*" *Essays on Shakespeare and Elizabethan Drama* (n. 3 above); repr. in Frye's *Fables of Identity* (New York, 1963).

41For a skeptical examination of "the Christian Shakespeare" see Roland M. Frye, *Shakespeare and Christian Doctrine* (Princeton, 1963).

42Some miscellaneous references for Orpheus are (1) Ancient: W. K. C. Guthrie, *Orpheus and Greek Religion: A Study of the Orphic Movement* (London, 1935; rev. 1952; New York, 1966); I. M. Linforth, *The Arts of Orpheus* (Berkeley, 1941); E. R. Dodds (below, III, n. 32); E. Ehnmark, "Some Notes on the Greek Orpheus Tradition," *Culture in History: Essays in Honor of Paul Radin,* ed. S. Diamond (New York, 1960); J. Pollard (below, III, n. 32), chap. 5, "The Followers of Orpheus," pp. 93-105; (2) Medieval and Modern: L. E. Marshall, "Greek Myths in Modern English Poetry: Orpheus and Eurydice," *Studi di Filologia Moderna* 5 (1912): pp. 203-232; 6 (1913): pp. 1-32; J. Wirl, *Orpheus in der englischen Literatur* (Wiener Beiträge 40, 1913); A. H. Gayton, "The Orpheus Myth in North America," *Journal of American Folk Lore* 48 (1935): pp. 263-286; F. A. Yates, *French Academies* (n. 34 above), *passim*, e.g., p. 64 and references; D. P. Walker, "Orpheus the Theologian and Renaissance Platonists," *JWCI* 16 (1953): pp. 100-110; Elizabeth Sewell, *The Orphic Voice* (New Haven, 1960); D. C. Allen, "Milton and the Descent to Light," *JEGP* 60 (1961): pp. 614-630; M. O. Lee (above, Preface, n. 1); D. J. McMillan, "Classical Tale plus Folk Tale," *American Notes and Queries* 3 (1962-1963): pp. 117-118, on Henryson's poem; *Sir Orfeo,* ed. A. J. Bliss (2nd ed. Oxford, 1966); K. R. Gros Louis, "Robert Henryson's *Orpheus and Eurydice* and the Orpheus Tradition of the Middle Ages," *Speculum* 41 (1966): pp. 643-655.

mentary, stressed the power of music to agitate or compose the affections. Alexander Ross elaborated what the church father, Clement of Alexandria, had said some fourteen centuries earlier: that "Christ is the true Orpheus," whose music drew the Gentiles to follow him, "who went down to hell, to recover the Church his Spouse," and suffered a cruel death.[43] That conception had been glanced at in *Christ's Victory and Triumph* (iii.7), by the clergyman Giles Fletcher, a poet who had some influence on Milton. Milton did not apparently accept the typological Orpheus, but his successive references rise from the simple Ovidian tale to reverberating symbolism and mark notable stages in his poetic career. The parallel allusions in *L'Allegro* and *Il Penseroso*, respectively happy and sombre, are only lyrical examples of different kinds of music. We have already noticed, in *Lycidas*, the central and harsh significance of the death of the archetypal poet. When in *Paradise Lost* the scene changes from hell to heaven, Milton recalls the downward and upward journeys of Orpheus and Aeneas and distinguishes his Christian work from pagan poetry: he sings "With other notes than to th'Orphean lyre." Midway in the poem, the poet who had given nearly twenty years and his eyesight to the Puritan revolution, now nullified by the restoration of Charles II, still seeks the guidance of his Heavenly Muse, though he is

> fall'n on evil days,
> On evil days though fall'n, and evil tongues;
> In darkness, and with dangers compassed round,
> And solitude. . . .

And again, with an oblique personal reference like that in *Lycidas*, and in similarly strident lines, he remembers the fate of Orpheus, of poetry, in an ugly world (vii.32 f.):

---

[43]Clement of Alexandria, *Exhortation to the Greeks*, etc. (Loeb Classical Library), pp. 9 f., 37, 43, 167; Alexander Ross, *Mystagogus Poeticus* (ed. 1648), pp. 334-337; D. C. Allen, *JEGP* 60 (1961): pp. 618-619; H. Spevack-Husmann (n. 44 below), pp. 81-88.

But drive far off the barbarous dissonance
Of Bacchus and his revelers, the race
Of that wild rout that tore the Thracian bard
In Rhodope, where woods and rocks had ears
To rapture, till the savage clamor drowned
Both harp and voice; nor could the Muse defend
Her son. So fail not thou who thee implores;
For thou art heav'nly, she an empty dream.

Paradise Lost is of course full of allusions, open like this one, or veiled—the latter kind ranging from the Promethean strain in Satan down to the newly created Eve's gazing, like Narcissus, at her image in the pool; and even brief items may be rich in both texture and implication.[44] But we must turn to our last mythological symbol.

We commonly think of Cupid as a ubiquitous small figure in Renaissance paintings, or as the blind, irresponsible bow-boy of Mercutio and Shakespearian comedy (his blindness, by the way, was almost wholly postclassical). But he had more

---

[44]There are studies of Milton's debts to classical authors, and particular themes, passages, and allusions have received innumerable comments in annotated editions, individual articles and notes, and general criticism. Much basic material is supplied in Charles G. Osgood, *The Classical Mythology of Milton's English Poems* (New York, 1900; repr. 1964). Some later discussions are: D. Bush, *Renaissance Tradition* (1963), pp. 260-297, with a bibliography; Walter F. Schirmer, *Antike, Renaissance*, etc. (Bibliography, I, below); Davis P. Harding, *Milton and the Renaissance Ovid* (Urbana, 1948), and *The Club of Hercules: Studies in the Classical Background of Paradise Lost* (Urbana, 1962); Helga Spevack-Husmann, *The Mighty Pan: Miltons Mythologische Vergleiche* (Münster, 1963); M. Y. Hughes, "'Devils to Adore for Deities,'" *Studies in Honor of DeWitt T. Starnes*, ed. James Sledd, T. P. Harrison, *et al.* (Austin, 1967), pp. 241-258. The chief discussion of one topic, R. J. Z. Werblowsky's *Lucifer and Prometheus: A Study of Milton's Satan* (London, 1952), invites continual disagreement. The chapter (pp. 226-340) on Milton in Starnes and Talbert (Bibliography, I, below) is perhaps more useful for the mythological data currently and readily available than in showing Milton's "sources," since one does not think of so learned a poet as likely to turn to dictionaries. Isabel G. MacCaffrey's *Paradise Lost as "Myth"* (Cambridge, Mass., 1959) is concerned with "myth" in the broad modern sense rather than with classical myth *per se*.

exalted roles.[45] Even as god of love the Cupid who kindled
passion in Jove and other deities was all-powerful and often
cruel. To quote Ben Jonson's *Haddington Masque,*

> At his sight the sun hath turned,
> Neptune in the waters burned;
> Hell hath felt a greater heat;
> Jove himself forsook his seat:
> From the centre to the sky
> Are his trophies reared high.

His many conquests are displayed in tapestry to Spenser's Brit-
omart (*Faerie Queene* III.xi.28 f.); she also witnesses a masque
of Cupid (III.xii.5 f.), which presents, not the ecstasies of
romantic and sensual love, but the pangs and griefs that attend
it. So strong is the tradition—so strong too the tradition of
poetic decorum—that the soberly Christian Spenser, in his
Hymn in Honor of Love, can address Cupid as "My guide, my
God, my victor, and my king." On a still higher plane the Neo-
platonic Cupid is the great cosmic force of love which at the
creation ranged the discordant elements of chaos in order. This
mighty Cupid Spenser saluted at length in the same *Hymn;*
but in the corresponding *Hymn of Heavenly Love* the Neo-
platonic account of creation only introduced the main theme,
a reverent and tender story of the life, suffering, and death of
Christ the Redeemer. The cosmic tradition was given a scientific twist in Bacon's interpretation of Cupid as the natural
motion of the atom. Still another kind of Platonic Cupid was
descended from Apuleius' tale of Cupid and Psyche, and for

---

[45]Some references for Cupid are: Adolf Hoffmann, *Das Psyche-Märchen des
Apuleius in der englischen Literatur* (Strassburg, 1908); J. Hutton, "The
First Idyl of Moschus in Imitations to the Year 1800," *American Journal of
Philology* **49** (1928): pp. 105-136; "Additions" to Hutton by J. G. Fucilla,
ibid. **50** (1929): pp. 190-193; Fucilla, "Materials for the History of a Popular
Classical Theme," *Classical Philology* **26** (1931): pp. 135-152; F. A. Spencer,
"The Literary Lineage of Cupid," *Classical Weekly* **25** (1931-1932): pp. 121-127,
139-144; E. Panofsky, "Blind Cupid," *Studies in Iconology* (below, Bibliography,
I), pp. 95-128; Alice Nearing, ed., *Cupid and Psyche, by Shakerly Marmion*
(Philadelphia, 1944), pp. 11-95; D. C. Allen, "On Spenser's *Muiopotmos,*" *SP*
53 (1956): pp. 141-158, who gives on pp. 146-149 a succinct summary of the
allegorical tradition; J. Espiner-Scott, "Les Sonnets élisabéthains: Cupidon et
l'influence d'Ovide," *RLC* **31** (1957): pp. 421-426; Edgar Wind, *Pagan
Mysteries* (below, Bibliography, I), chap. 4; Robert Ellrodt, *Neoplatonism in
the Poetry of Spenser* (Geneva, 1960); Thomas P. Roche, *The Kindly Flame:
A Study of the Third and Fourth Books of Spenser's Faerie Queene* (Princeton,
1964), *passim.*

illustrations we turn to two Christian Platonists, Spenser and his greatest disciple.

One of Spenser's most elaborate and philosophic myths is that of the Garden of Adonis (*Faerie Queene*, III.vi).[46] The immediate occasion is that it is in this Garden that Amoret, a type of ideal woman and wife, is brought up by Psyche. The canto begins with the miraculous conception and the birth of Amoret and her twin sister, and with the light traditional motif of Venus' search for her wayward son Cupid. But it turns into a generalized, abstract myth of creation akin to Plato's. The Garden is the seed-bed of forms and matter, from which bodies are framed and sent into the world and to which they return to be planted and created again. It is a quite naturalistic picture of a cycle of physical generation except for one significant echo of Genesis (III.vi.34) : the whole process obeys the word first spoken by God. Spenser then embodies the idea in a particular myth, the perpetual love of Venus, who is matter, and Adonis, the father of all forms. Although the peace of the Garden is threatened by Time, Spenser is able here to contemplate without disquiet an ordered world of becoming. Along with Venus and Adonis in this paradise are Cupid and Psyche, whose daughter, Pleasure, is the companion of Amoret. It was apparently this Spenserian myth of Venus and Adonis, of physical generation, that Milton had in mind in his allusion in the epilogue of *Comus*;[47] there Venus and Adonis are placed below Cupid and Psyche, whose progeny are Youth and Joy—

---

[46]For interpretations of Spenser's Garden of Adonis some references are: commentaries in the Variorum Edition; M. Miller, "Nature in the *Faerie Queene*," *ELH* 18 (1951) : pp. 191-200; R. Ellrodt, *Neoplatonism* (n. 45 above) ; C. S. Lewis' elaborate review of Ellrodt, *Études Anglaises* 14 (1961) : pp. 107-116 (repr. in Lewis' *Studies in Medieval and Renaissance Literature* (Cambridge, 1966)) ; H. Berger, "Spenser's Gardens of Adonis: Force and Form in the Renaissance Imagination," *UTQ* 30 (1960-1961) : pp. 128-149; William Nelson, *The Poetry of Edmund Spenser* (New York, 1963) , pp. 204-235; T. P. Roche (n. 45 above) , pp. 96-128, etc.; Judith C. Ramsay, "The Garden of Adonis and the Garden of Forms," *UTQ* 35 (1965-1966) : pp. 188-206; Donald Cheney, *Spenser's Image of Nature* (New Haven, 1966) , pp. 117-145; Rosalie L. Colie, *Paradoxa Epidemica* (Princeton, 1966) , pp. 329-341; A. B. Giamatti (n. 5 above) , pp. 284-290; K. Williams (n. 17 above) , pp. 145-150, etc.; F. Kermode, *The Sense of an Ending* (New York, 1967) , pp. 74-78; P. J. Alpers (n. 23 above) , pp. 5-8, etc.

[47]Woodhouse, "The Argument of Milton's *Comus*" (n. 25 above) .

not what the sensual Comus claimed but, as we observed before, the true freedom that goes with virtue and leads to heaven.

The inexorable process of time and change haunted the Renaissance imagination and inspired much of its finest poetry and prose, and Spenser returned to the theme in his last and perhaps greatest cantos, on Mutability. Here the problem of flux and permanence has a different focus and is far more disturbing than it was in the Garden of Adonis. The matrix of Spenser's mythic invention is the war of the gods and Titans. The Titaness Mutability has gained sway on earth, corrupting the original perfect creation—an implicit fusion of Adam's fall and the classical myth of decay from the golden age. Now, challenging the rule of Jove and the other gods, Mutability claims dominion in heaven as well as on earth. Her case is heard before the supreme deity, Nature, who is clearly a surrogate for God, and whose sergeant is Order. The Titaness, in proof of her claim, brings forth a pageant of the seasons, months, day and night, the hours, and life and death.[48] Nature's

---

[48]Sherman Hawkins has argued that the regular sequence of the months and their realistic and symbolic character constitute an assertion of order ("Mutabilitie and the Cycle of the Months," *Form and Convention in the Poetry of Edmund Spenser*, ed. William Nelson (New York, 1961), pp. 76-102). This view had been briefly stated by Northrop Frye *(Anatomy of Criticism* (Princeton, 1957), p. 204; and in *Myth and Mythmaking*, ed. Henry A. Murray (New York, 1960), p. 125). It is endorsed by Mr. Nelson in his own excellent book (n. 46 above), pp. 304, 336; by W. Blissett, "Spenser's Mutabilitie," *Essays in English Literature . . . Presented to A. S. P. Woodhouse*, ed. M. MacLure and F. Watt (Toronto, 1964), pp. 26-42; and K. Williams, *Spenser's World of Glass* (n. 17 above), p. 229. Mr. Blissett remarks that, "quite apart from the promise of eternity, Nature and the poet's Muse look upon the mutable world itself with calmness and joy" (p. 42; *cf.* Hawkins, pp. 88 f.). Whatever Spenser's delight in the mutable world, I am quite unable to see how Mutability, as "the victim of a vast dramatic irony" (Hawkins, p. 87), could be made to thus undercut her own argument (and Spenser's view of her in VII. vi. 4-7 or his proem to Book V) and thereby turn Nature's judgment and above all the anguished last stanzas into a weak and illogical anticlimax. See Thomas Greene, *The Descent from Heaven* (New Haven, 1963), pp. 322-323, and, e.g., M. Miller, D. Cheney (pp. 239-247), R. L. Colie (pp. 341-352), and F. Kermode (pp. 78-81), all cited in n. 46 above. See also R. Ringler, "The Faunus Episode," *MP* 63 (1961-1962): pp. 12-19; Jean MacIntyre, "Artegall's Sword and the Mutabilitie Cantos," *ELH* 33 (1966): pp. 405-414; and Joanne F. Holland, "The Cantos of Mutabilitie and the Form of *The Faerie Queene*," *ELH* 35 (1968): pp. 21-31.

Spenser's use of Ovid in these cantos was set forth by W. P. Cumming, *SP* 28 (1931): pp. 241-256; *cf.* Lotspeich (n. 17 above), "Mutability" (both are summarized in the Variorum Edition of *The Faerie Queene: Books VI and VII*, pp. 408-410).

verdict is in the tradition of Christian naturalism: there is continual change, though it is not haphazard flux; it is evolution
under Providence.[49] But there follow two stanzas in which,
while he does accept the traditional Christian solution, Spenser
is still so overwhelmed by the fact of incessant change that, in
the spirit of *contemptus mundi*, he utters an anguished prayer
for the eternal stability of heaven:

> When I bethinke me on that speech whyleare,
>   Of Mutability, and well it way:
>   Me seemes, that though she all unworthy were
>   Of the Heav'ns Rule; yet very sooth to say,
>   In all things else she beares the greatest sway.
>   Which makes me loath this state of life so tickle,
>   And love of things so vaine to cast away;
>   Whose flowring pride, so fading and so fickle,
> Short Time shall soon cut down with his consuming sickle.
>
> Then gin I thinke on that which Nature sayd,
>   Of that same time when no more Change shall be,
>   But stedfast rest of all things firmely stayd
>   Upon the pillours of Eternity,
>   That is contrayr to Mutabilitie:
>   For, all that moveth, doth in Change delight:
>   But thence-forth all shall rest eternally
>   With Him that is the God of Sabbaoth hight:
> O that great Sabbaoth God, graunt me that Sabaoths sight.

There is here a partial affinity with *Paradise Lost*. The
whole body of Milton's verse and prose was inspired by a vision
of perfection. In his early poems, up through *Lycidas,* that perfection was heaven. In his many prose tracts Milton labored
toward the establishment of Christ's kingdom, something like
heaven, on earth. In *Paradise Lost,* finished when the Puritan
revolution had finally failed, the dream of a new reformation

---

[49]Medieval conceptions of nature are discussed, e.g., by E. R. Curtius (below,
Bibliography, I), pp. 106-127; K. Svendsen, *Milton and Science* (Cambridge,
Mass., 1956), *passim;* C. S. Lewis, *The Discarded Image* (Cambridge, 1964). On
Mutabilitie and medieval tradition see the commentary in the Variorum Edition
(n. 48 above), especially B. Stirling, pp. 416-419, 421-422; C. S. Lewis, *Allegory
of Love,* pp. 353-357 (quoted in Variorum Ed., pp. 427-429), and *Studies* (n.
46 above), p. 152; and a number of references in nn. 23, 46, 48, and 49 above.
For a contemporary parallel to Spenser's view of the religio-metaphysical
question, see the debate between the pious Pamela and the atheistic Cecropia
in Sidney's *Arcadia*, ed. Feuillerat (Cambridge, 1912), pp. 402-410.

and of Christ's second coming has given way to a now remote vision of the eternity of perfection that will follow the day of judgment. Meanwhile, we see what fallen man has lost. Into his picture of the garden home of Adam and Eve, Milton pours all the traditional features of earthly paradises and the golden age; for Eden (like hell and heaven) is not only a place but a state of mind, an outward symbol of total beauty, innocence, and harmony.[50] Such a vision of perfection naturally draws upon classical myth. Here

>   universal Pan,
> Knit with the Graces and the Hours in dance,
> Led on th'eternal spring. Not that fair field
> Of Enna, where Proserpine gathering flow'rs,
> Herself a fairer flow'r, by gloomy Dis
> Was gathered, which cost Ceres all that pain
> To seek her through the world . . .
> . . . . might with this Paradise
> Of Eden strive. . . .

This simile, with its poignant suggestion of mortal beauty and loss and its implied anticipation of the fate of Eve, is surely the most complex and beautiful in English poetry. It is, for the present, a final reminder that the old myths are never worn out except by poor poets; they can always be powerfully re-created by a great one.

This has been a sketchy survey of a vast and varied body of material; and it has seemed good to cite many familiar things, just because their familiarity is the best evidence of their poetic vitality. At any rate it should be clear that in the poetry of

---

[50]A recent and suggestive discussion of Milton's Eden is in A. B. Giamatti (n. 5 above), who, as usual, gives abundant references. A few other discussions are: Paul Elmer More, "The Theme of 'Paradise Lost,'" *Shelburne Essays, Fourth Series* (New York, 1906), pp. 139-153; Arnold Stein, *Answerable Style* (Minneapolis, 1953), pp. 52-74; W. G. Madsen (n. 25 above), pp. 218-283; I. G. MacCaffrey (n. 44 above), especially pp. 149-157; F. Kermode, "Adam Unparadised," *The Living Milton*, ed. Kermode (London, 1960), pp. 85-123; D. P. Harding, *The Club of Hercules* (n. 44 above), pp. 67-85; Joseph H. Summers, *The Muse's Method: An Introduction to Paradise Lost* (Cambridge, Mass., 1962); Anne D. Ferry, *Milton's Epic Voice (ibid.,* 1963), *passim;* Stanley E. Fish, *Surprised by Sin: The Reader in Paradise Lost* (London and New York, 1967); H. Berger, "*Paradise Lost* Evolving: Books i-vi," *Centennial Review* 11 (1967): pp. 483-531.

the Renaissance images and symbols drawn from classical myth were, more than in any period before or since, an instinctive, native language. And we have observed some reasons for that: the classical education of almost all who wrote and read; a traditional way of life still close to the rhythms and forces of nature; a religious or "magical" view of the world, a world still full of supernatural presences. In that world everything was related by analogy and correspondence to everything else, because there was one all-embracing body of natural and supernatural truth which could both assess and assimilate pagan fiction.

II. The Romantic Revival

MILTON'S HANDLING of classical myth was the peak of Renaissance art, but he, a more exclusively religious poet than Spenser, was more impelled to distinguish Christian truth from pagan fiction. The Reformation and the Counter-Reformation had revived some old antipathies toward mythological art and poetry, although in Europe generally these were not fatal. In England hostility was not merely Puritan or merely religious but was also literary and rationalistic. In the middle of the seventeenth century the royalist poet Abraham Cowley, who was best known for his amatory verse, declared in favor of Biblical themes against "confused antiquated Dreams of senseless Fables and Metamorphoses."[1] Sir William Davenant and Hobbes opposed all imaginative fictions that dealt with the fabulous and preternatural and prescribed for poetry the realistic treatment of men and manners.[2] Both the negative and the positive sides of this reaction were strengthened by the conspicuous growth of science and the cool critical rationalism that attended it. An increasingly prominent strain in religious thought was Deism, and its general temper might be inferred from the title of one book, *Christianity Not Mysterious* (1696), by the admiring editor of Milton's libertarian prose, John Toland. Then, in Europe at large, from the late seventeenth century onward the imaginative and allegorical conceptions of myth, which had been so closely bound up with great poetry, gave way largely to sophisticated historical inquiries into the origins and real nature of myth, the psychology of primitive societies, and comparative religion. This rationalistic and skeptical movement, carried on by such notable figures as Pierre

---

[1]Cowley, preface to his *Poems* (1656), in *Critical Essays of the Seventeenth Century*, ed. J. E. Spingarn (Oxford, 1908-1909), 2: p. 88.

[2]For Davenant and Hobbes see Spingarn (n. 1 above), 2: pp. 2, 4-5, etc.

Bayle and Fontenelle and others, was a substantial part of the eighteenth-century Enlightenment.[3]

Such changing attitudes had quite logical consequences in poetry, both Continental and English. In the later two-thirds of the seventeenth century one minor but not insignificant phenomenon was the writing of travesties, more often crude than clever, of ancient epics and tales.[4] A much larger fact was the dominance, in the Augustan age, of satire, as the names of Dryden and Pope remind us. Poetical theory and practice excluded or subdued the imaginative and visionary faculties which earlier and later generations of poets and readers prized more highly than the rationalistic and realistic. Moreover, the texture of poetry, in keeping with its climate and aims, had changed from the varied, concrete, metaphorical, and suggestive language of the Renaissance poets to a more uniform diction and syntax that favored the denotative, the general, and the abstract. Reverence for classical art and classical wisdom remained, but classical myths either disappeared or became as pallid as the personified abstractions that took their place.[5] We remember the grounds of Dr. Johnson's hostility, expressed in his comments on *Lycidas* and elsewhere. Only one or two poets, notably William Collins, had an imagination primitive enough to vitalize myths. In the whole range of eighteenth-century verse there is perhaps no classical allusion equal in imaginative resonance to Gibbon's account of his first conceiving of his history, as in Rome, in 1764, he "sat musing amidst the ruins of the Capitol, while the bare-footed fryars

---

3See A. J. Kuhn, F. E. Manuel, A. Zwerdling, and P. Gay, in the Bibliography, II, below.

4A brief sketch of travesties, with references, is given in D. Bush, *Renaissance Tradition* (1963) , pp. 298-305.

5Eighteenth-century responses—so different from ours—are discussed by, e.g., B. H. Bronson, "Personification Reconsidered," *ELH* 14 (1947) : pp. 163-177; enlarged in *New Light on Dr. Johnson*, ed. F. W. Hilles (New Haven, 1959) , pp. 189-231; E. R. Wasserman, *PMLA* 65 (1950) : pp. 435-463; R. Trickett (below, Bibliography, II) , who is concerned also with classical mythology; Chester F. Chapin, *Personification in Eighteenth-Century English Poetry* (New York, 1955) ; Patricia M. Spacks, *SP* 59 (1962) : pp. 560-578. For the general background see W. J. Bate, *From Classic to Romantic: Premises of Taste in Eighteenth-Century England* (Cambridge, Mass., 1946) , and M. H. Abrams (n. 16 below) .

were singing vespers in the Temple of Jupiter."[6] During the Romantic age the growth of skeptical rationalism, of science and technology and industrialism, continued to alter traditional ways of life and the "magical" view of the world that had persisted since ancient Judea and Greece. Within one decade such diverse witnesses as Hazlitt, Keats, Peacock, Macaulay, and Tennyson bore reluctant testimony to the doctrine that poetry, in its nature a primitive thing, was bound to decay as civilization advanced.[7]

However, just as skeptical rationalism had been growing while the exalted Renaissance conception of poetry was strongest, so the Romantic reaction was growing throughout the so-called age of reason; and we remember that the Romantic movement was not merely literary and artistic but involved a radical change in values and in direction, a transformation of thought, feeling, and action in all areas of life. While humanitarians abhorred the obvious and ugly effects of political oppression or of the industrial revolution, the most fundamental reaction was against the scientific, mechanistic view of both the external universe and the human psyche. We recall the names of Blake's evil trinity, Bacon, Newton, and Locke. Whereas Newton's successors had made his divine cosmos into a machine, the Romantic poets felt impelled toward a concept of dynamic wholeness and unity that embraced the universe, terrestrial nature, and man; and in that intuition they were decidedly in advance of mechanistic scientists.[8] So too microcosmic man was

---

[6]*Memoirs of the Life of Edward Gibbon,* ed. G. B. Hill (London, 1900), p. 167. As a safeguard against an unduly romantic reading of the sentence, one might quote Paul Fussell: "The detail of the friars is a master touch, suggesting as it does Gibbon's whole theme, 'the triumph of barbarism and Christianity'" (*The Rhetorical World of Augustan Humanism* (Oxford, 1965), p. 201).

[7]Hazlitt, "The English Poets," *Works,* ed. P. P. Howe (London, 1930-1934), 5: p. 9; Keats, *Lamia,* ii. 229 f. (*cf.* the toast drunk at Haydon's "immortal dinner," described, after Haydon, by Keats's biographers, e.g., W. J. Bate, *John Keats* (Cambridge, Mass., 1963), p. 270); *Peacock's Four Ages of Poetry,* etc., ed. H. F. B. Brett-Smith (Boston, 1921), pp. 15 f.; Macaulay, "Milton," *Critical and Historical Essays . . . by Lord Macaulay,* ed. F. C. Montague (London, 1903), 1: p. 91; Tennyson, *Timbuctoo* (1829), lines 215-245. The young Macaulay may have been echoing Hazlitt (P. L. Carver, *RES 6* (1930): p. 61) or, more probably, Peacock (F. L. Jones, *Modern Language Quarterly* 13 (1952): pp. 356-362).

[8]Alfred N. Whitehead, *Science and the Modern World* (New York, 1925), pp. 104-133.

an individual whole, a person, not—as Matthew Arnold was to protest in his sonnet on Butler's sermons—a fixed, mechanical aggregate of "Affections, Instincts, Principles, and Powers." In regard to these grand questions, we may remember that English poets of the Renaissance had been more or less devout Christians for whom a providential world-order and heaven and hell were prime matters of belief, while the Romantic poets stood more or less outside orthodox faith and had to grope toward valid and usable philosophies of their own. Another general fact, of high importance for the whole modern period, first became a fact in the Romantic age: that is, the alienation of the poet, the artist, from the mass of society and his consciousness of that alienation. For one large example, the French Revolution sharply divided the small minority of enthusiastic liberals and radicals (the poets among them) from the conservative or reactionary majority.

The revival of myth was a logical part of the Romantic movement, and, in particular, of the "Romantic Hellenism" that was European and especially German,[9] but in England it developed in its own way, with much less storm and stress. The early eighteenth century revealed the first distinct signs of a new orientation toward Greece rather than Rome as the great nursery of art, literature, and liberty.[10] Growing interest in Greek archaeology and in what was supposed to be classical Greek sculpture led eventually to battle over the Elgin Marbles, in which Keats's friend, Haydon the painter, took a vigorous share.[11] There was, too, growing interest in folklore and ballads, and Thomas Blackwell's idea of Homer as a wandering

[9]The Bibliography, II, below, lists a broad sketch of Romantic Hellenism by Harry Levin and books on France and Germany by R. Canat and H. Hatfield, who give full references. See also n. 24 below for writings on Prometheus.

For general discussion and bibliographies of the younger English Romantic poets see Ian Jack, *English Literature 1815-1832* (Oxford History of English Literature, 10 (1963)), and *English Romantic Writers*, ed. David Perkins (New York, 1967).

[10]On the rise of Hellenism in England see S. A. Larrabee, J. M. Osborn, and B. H. Stern (below, Bibliography, II) and T. J. B. Spencer (*ibid.*, General, and n. 26 below).

[11]The chief accounts of the Elgin Marbles are: A. H. Smith, "Lord Elgin and His Collection," *Journal of Hellenic Studies* 36 (1916): pp. 163-372, and William St. Clair, *Lord Elgin and the Marbles* (London, 1967). See also S. A. Larrabee (Bibliography, II, below) and Ian Jack (n. 29 below).

bard resulted, at the end of the century, in Wolf's posing of "the Homeric question," a question still much debated. In another book (1748) Blackwell enthusiastically expounded mythology as the first religion and philosophy of man. We noted early unsophisticated efforts to relate classical myth to the Bible, and this kind of inquiry was zealously pursued, in more sophisticated terms, from the later seventeenth century onward, along with the continuance of skeptical researches.[12] Both Christian and anti-Christian scholars, for opposed reasons, sought in myth the key to a primordial unity in the religious experience and imagination of the human race. (Of such syncretists George Eliot's misguided Mr. Casaubon is a fictional representative.) This activity covered all ancient myth and religion, from the East Indians to the Druids, and yielded a great deal of often wild speculation which seems to have had little direct influence on any of the major Romantic poets except Blake.[13] But even these works attested the serious importance of myth, and there were more disinterested aids to literary

---

[12]See the references in n. 3 above.

[13]Accounts of this body of writings, with more or less reference to Blake, are: E. B. Hungerford and A. J. Kuhn (Bibliography, II, below); Ruthven Todd, "William Blake and the Eighteenth-Century Mythologists," *Tracks in the Snow: Studies in English Science and Art* (London and New York, 1947), pp. 29-60; Northrop Frye, *Fearful Symmetry: A Study of William Blake* (Princeton, 1947), pp. 108-144, 173 f. Frye (pp. 108-109) quotes Blake on the Bible and classical myth: "Let it here be noted that the Greek Fables originated in Spiritual Mystery & Real Vision, which are lost & clouded in Fable & Allegory, while the Hebrew Bible & the Greek Gospel are Genuine, Preserv'd by the Saviour's Mercy" (*Vision of the Last Judgment*, in *The Writings of William Blake*, ed. Sir G. Keynes (London, 1925), 3: p. 146). Cf. Frye, pp. 119-120, 124, 131-132, 155 f.

It is perhaps needless to say that my sketch leaves out Blake because that apocalyptic rebel abominated the classics as identified with war and the establishment and created his own mythology—although (as Frye, e.g., shows) it contained disguised elements of classical myth. While Blake has become a name to conjure with, I venture to think that an esoteric mythology, which has to be got up like so much Gothic, suffers immeasurably in contrast with classical myths that retain their identity and suggestive power through all their poetic incarnations.

I may add that Landor—not to speak of many lesser poets—is left out because, though he retold many myths and tales in carefully chiseled English (and Latin), he had next to nothing to say. There is no room for Browning, whose considerable and (apart from *Artemis Prologizes*) characteristic dealings with mythology do not include any of his best poems. He is discussed in my *Romantic Tradition*, pp. 358-385; and see W. C. De Vane and R. Spindler (below, Bibliography, II).

rehabilitation. It will be enough to mention a few books, old and new and diverse in spirit, which have become familiar to us because they were eagerly absorbed by the young or the mature Keats. These were Andrew Tooke's rudimentary *Pantheon* (1698); John Potter's large account of Greek antiquities (1697-1699), which Keats used especially in *Lamia;* Joseph Spence's *Polymetis* (1747; abridged edition, 1764 f.); John Lempriere's *Classical Dictionary* (1788 and later editions); and the *Pantheon* (1806) by "Edward Baldwin," i.e. William Godwin, the hard-headed author of that very influential work of doctrinaire radicalism, *Political Justice.* Godwin, it may be observed, treats Greek myth seriously as a religion.[14] Keats also used the richly suggestive Ovidian commentary of George Sandys, which we noticed before; the connection reminds us that traditional allegory could readily pass into modern symbolism. Keats's ardent responsiveness to classical myth also reminds us that conservative opinion—sufficiently represented by the review of Keats by Francis Jeffrey, the editor of the powerful *Edinburgh Review*[15]—continued to deplore the poetic use of such material; and Tennyson and Arnold were to encounter the rising demand for wholly modern subject matter, a demand Arnold opposed in the important preface to his *Poems* of 1853.

To return to the center of the Romantic scene, the testimony of Coleridge and Wordsworth implies that the main initial agent in the revitalizing of Greek myth was the Romantic religion of nature, if that loose old phrase will serve to characterize their reaction against the mechanistic view of the world and man. Coleridge did not himself use mythology in his poems, at least not in his good ones, but in his translation of Schiller's *Wallenstein* he enlarged the original with lines which sum up his nostalgic feeling:

---

[14]Zwerdling *(PMLA 79* (1964) : pp. 453-455; *UTQ 33* (1963-1964) : pp. 343-344: see below, Bibliography, II, and n. 22) calls attention to the serious views of Greek myth as a religion or metaphysics in Godwin's *Pantheon* and Richard Payne Knight's *Inquiry into the Symbolical Language of Ancient Art and Mythology* (1818).

[15]Jeffrey's review *(Edinburgh Review* 34 (1820) : pp. 203-213) is reprinted in *Jeffrey's Literary Criticism,* ed. D. Nichol Smith (London, 1910), and *Complete Poetry and Selected Prose of John Keats,* ed. H. E. Briggs (New York, 1951).

> The intelligible forms of ancient poets,
> The fair humanities of old religion,
> The Power, the Beauty, and the Majesty,
> That had their haunts in dale, or piny mountain,
> Or forest by slow stream, or pebbly spring,
> Or chasms and wat'ry depths; all these have vanished.
> They live no longer in the faith of reason!
> But still the heart doth need a language, still
> Doth the old instinct bring back the old names. . . .[16]

Or, as Peacock later said, more drily: "We know too that there are no Dryads in Hyde-park nor Naiads in the Regent's-canal."[17] But the religious Coleridge felt more than aesthetic nostalgia, as indeed the phrase "faith of reason" indicates. Later he protested that "the mechanical system of philosophy" had made the world in relation to God like a building in relation to its mason, and had left "the idea of omnipresence a mere abstract notion in the state-room of our reason."[18]

Corresponding to Coleridge's sense of God's omnipresence was Wordsworth's instinctive animism, which made him, even as a boy, feel mysterious presences and powers in natural objects and scenes.[19] Thus, while he avowedly had shared in the

---

[16]Coleridge, *Wallenstein,* Part I *(The Piccolomini),* II. iv. 123 f. *(Complete Poetical Works,* ed. E. H. Coleridge (Oxford, 1912) , 2: p. 649). Coleridge, however, could also say that to the Greek poets "All natural Objects were *dead*—mere hollow Statues—but there was a Godkin or Goddessling *included* in each. . . . At best, it is but Fancy, or the aggregating Faculty of the mind— not *Imagination,* or the *modifying,* and *co-adunating* Faculty. . . . In the Hebrew Poets each Thing has a Life of it's own, & yet they are all one Life." Letter to Sotheby, September 10, 1802, *Letters,* ed. E. L. Griggs, 2 (Oxford, 1956) : pp. 865-866. See M. H. Abrams, *The Mirror and the Lamp* (New York, 1953, 1958) , pp. 290-297.

[17]*Peacock's Four Ages of Poetry* (n. 7 above) , p. 15.

[18]Coleridge, *Biographia Literaria,* ed. J. Shawcross (Oxford, 1907) , 2: p. 59 n.

[19]Wordsworth's "animism" (a quality of vision known by other names) has been more or less discussed by many critics, e.g.: Melvin M. Rader, "Presiding Ideas in Wordsworth's Poetry," *University of Washington Publications in Language and Literature* 8 (1931) : pp. 121-215; J. W. Beach, *The Concept of Nature in Nineteenth-Century English Poetry* (New York, 1936) ; R. D. Havens, *The Mind of a Poet* (Baltimore, 1941) ; D. Ferry, *The Limits of Mortality* (Middletown, 1959) ; D. Perkins, *The Quest for Permanence* (below, Bibliography, II) , and *Wordsworth and the Poetry of Sincerity* (Cambridge, Mass., 1964) ; J. Benziger (below, Bibliography, II) ; H. W. Piper, *The Active Universe: Pantheism and the concept of Imagination in the English Romantic Poets* (London, 1962) ; G. H. Hartman, *Wordsworth's Poetry 1787-1814* (New Haven, 1964) ; C. Woodring, *Wordsworth* (Boston, 1965) ; Melvin Rader, *Wordsworth: A Philosophical Approach* (Oxford, 1967) .

eighteenth century's "disgust"[20] with poetical mythology, his animistic imagination could at times find a degree of spiritual health in the local divinities and pieties of Greek myth. The most stirring and familiar example is the sonnet, "The world is too much with us." Here the spectacle of a nominally Christian nation, unaware of nature and greedily intent on war-time "Getting and spending," inspires the outburst:

> Great God! I'd rather be
> A Pagan suckled in a creed outworn;
> So might I, standing on this pleasant lea,
> Have glimpses that would make me less forlorn;
> Have sight of Proteus rising from the sea;
> Or hear old Triton blow his wreathèd horn.

It may seem a very limited eulogy to say that even "a creed outworn" is better than the Christian worship of Mammon; but Wordsworth's vehemence goes beyond strict logic. The images of Proteus and Triton, by the way, come from Spenser,[21] and the echoes are a small reminder that the mature Wordsworth and Keats and Shelley more or less leaped over eighteenth-century verse to return to the older and more imaginative poets. Later, in the fourth book of *The Excursion*,[22]

---

[20]Wordsworth recorded his "disgust" in his note on his *Ode to Lycoris (Poetical Works,* ed. E. de Selincourt and H. Darbishire, Oxford, 4 (1947): pp. 422-423).

[21]Proteus was evidently suggested by lines 248-251 of *Colin Clout's Come Home Again (cf. Faerie Queene* III. viii and IV. xii), Triton's "wreathèd horn" and "pleasant lea" by lines 245 and 283.

[22]*Excursion* iv. 718-762, 847-887. Alex Zwerdling ("Wordsworth and Greek Myth," *UTQ* 33 (1963-1964): pp. 341-354) rightly emphasizes the Christian reservations that limit the poet's response but seems to me to somewhat exaggerate hostility and condescension and to miss the considerable warmth of sympathy that animates the two passages. He does not mention another passage, vi. 538-568, in which the Sceptic, citing the myths of Prometheus, Tantalus, and the line of Thebes, says that these fictions embody "Tremendous truths"—though the Priest rejects the "ruthless destiny" of pagan belief.

As possible sources of suggestions J. S. Lyon *(The Excursion: A Study* (New Haven, 1950), p. 59) mentions the passage in *The Piccolomini* (n. 16 above) and especially Schiller's lyric *Die Götter Griechenlands,* although Wordsworth's purpose is "entirely his own." Schiller seems rather unlikely for Wordsworth. Zwerdling (above) summarizes the attitudes of mythographers before and during Wordsworth's time, and notes (p. 344) that he owned the abridged *Polymetis,* Tooke, and two copies of Lempriere. Elisabeth K. Holmes *(MLN* 54 (1939): pp. 127-129) traced some bits on Middle-Eastern myths *(Excursion* iv. 671-678, 684-687, 689-699, 700, 709-711) to Samuel Purchas' *Purchas his Pilgrimage* (1614) and one (iv. 746-749) to Francis Rous's *Archaeologiae Atticae* (1642). Wordsworth owned both books.

Wordsworth had two long passages in which, in a similar but quieter vein, he described the Greek religion of nature and its symbolic meanings—now contrasted with what he had attacked in earlier poems, the desiccating pursuit of scientific analysis. Whatever Wordsworth's Christian reservations, these passages may be said to have provided a new basis and authority for the revival of myth in English poetry, most immediately for Keats. To mention one very different item, Wordsworth's rereading of Virgil with his son prompted a poem of exalted, semi-Virgilian style, *Laodamia*; its insistence, made increasingly stern in revision, on moral control of amorous passion has chilled many Wordsworthians, but it might have been approved (with reservations) by Spenser, Chapman, and Milton.[23]

The Renaissance poets had found in mythology a storehouse of moral examples good or bad, a symbolic language that was superhuman, timeless, universal. The younger generation of Romantic poets and their Victorian successors were moved by a similar idealism, an idealism, however, less concerned with traditional morality and more with the philosophizing of personal aspiration and vision. And, just as Coleridge, Hazlitt, Lamb, and Keats reinterpreted Shakespeare with a new inwardness, so Keats and Shelley re-created myths with a new, sometimes half-private, elaboration of symbolic meaning. And their own active senses, along with their response to Spenser, Shakespeare, and Milton and to painting and sculpture, resulted in mythological poetry of a sensuous luxuriance almost unapproached since the Renaissance poets.

We noticed the attraction that the moralized tale of Circe held for the Renaissance, and in the Romantic period one myth of equally characteristic significance was that of Prometheus, the Titan who—in different stories—created man out of clay or defied Zeus by giving man fire.[24] The re-creation of the

---

23In the tacitly Christian Platonism of *Laodamia* (139-149) Wordsworth seems to have remembered *Paradise Lost* viii. 586 f.; apparently he did not remember "Hail, wedded Love" (*ibid.*, iv. 750 f.) .

24The whole history of Prometheus in literature, from the beginning to the present, is magisterially treated by Raymond Trousson (see below, Bibliography, General) . Among many special studies are two by O. Walzel and C. Kreutz (Bibliography II) and one by O. Raggio (*ibid.*, General) . Many writings are listed in the full bibliographies of Trousson and Kreutz; the former's work includes much on the mythological tradition in general.

mythic culture-hero followed two main lines. One was the conception of Prometheus as the archetype of the free creative
artist, the original genius, the half-divine "maker." This high
notion of the creative fire of the Promethean poet, congenial
to such Renaissance Platonists as Chapman and the young
Milton,[25] was given an influential formulation by Lord Shaftesbury in the early eighteenth century, and developed, with increasing human assertiveness, up through Goethe and beyond.
The other conception, more familiar and more enduring, was
that of the heroic, isolated rebel against repressive authority,
divine and human. These interpretations, which could readily
merge together, symbolized and strengthened the Romantic
exalting of self-expression over neoclassical restraints, and, later
and more largely, the revolutionary struggle against political,
social, and religious oppression and reaction. The young
Goethe treated both conceptions of Prometheus, in a frag-
mentary drama and a monologue. And the creative and rebel-
lious Prometheus could be blended with Faust and Satan—
especially with a misreading of Milton's Satan—into a com-
posite, anti-Christian Titanism which was to gain a fresh im-
petus from Nietzsche.

Byron, the great English rebel, said that as a boy he had
been "passionately fond" of Aeschylus' *Prometheus Bound*, and
that the drama was always so much in his head that it might
easily have influenced all or anything he had written.[26] We
may take that remark as a compendious review of the various

---

[25]Trousson (1: p. 225) quotes Chapman on the creative fire of the "more-
then-humane soules" of "Promethean Poets" (*Hymnus in Noctem*, lines 131-133:
Poems of George Chapman, ed. P. B. Bartlett, New York, 1941, pp. 22-23).
Roy Battenhouse ("Chapman and the Nature of Man," *ELH* 12 (1945): p. 95)
remarks that "Chapman's Christ is . . . a Promethean poet" (quoted by M.
MacLure, *George Chapman*, p. 79). Trousson's Miltonic reference is apparently
to Milton's early *Ad Patrem* 20, on the poet "Sancta Prometheae retinens
vestigia flammae."

[26]*Letters and Journals of Lord Byron*, ed. R. E. Prothero (London and New
York, 1922-1924), 4: pp. 174-175. Most of Byron's allusions to Prometheus were
collected by S. C. Chew, *MLN* 33 (1918): pp. 306-309. He linked Prometheus
with Napoleon in his *Ode to Napoleon Buonaparte* (1814) and *The Age of
Bronze* (1823), lines 227 f.; see H. Bloom (below, Bibliography, II). For
Byron's literary Hellenism see, e.g., Harold Spender, *Byron and Greece* (London,
1924); D. Bush, *Romantic Tradition* (1937), pp. 71-80; T. J. B. Spencer's *Fair
Greece* (Bibliography, General, below) and his lecture of 1959, *Byron and the
Greek Tradition* (Nottingham).

Byronic heroes from Childe Harold up through Manfred, Don Juan, and Cain. But there is also the short monologue of 1816 in which Byron, with impressive force and dignity, makes the Titan the mouthpiece for his own defiance of the Calvinistic Deity whom he could neither obey nor forget. This strong, simple poem exemplifies the Romantic use of myth for the utterance of personal feeling, the adoption of a role or identity much more direct and complete than, say, Milton's allusions to Orpheus.

In Shelley's *Prometheus Unbound* (1818-1819) some qualities of the Romantic and Byronic Prometheus are spelled out, or changed, with a new fullness, depth, and subtlety.[27] Byron exalted the Titan's godlike kindness and endurance as well as his resistance, but, in keeping with his own ineradicable sense of sin, saw his hero as, like man,

> in part divine,
> A troubled stream from a pure source.

Shelley's drama, with all its complexities and occasional recognition of man's weakness of will, partakes of the simple idealism that sets pure white against pure black. He apparently did

---

[27]A full bibliography for Shelley is given by Ian Jack (1963: n. 9 above). *Shelley's Prometheus Unbound: A Variorum Edition,* ed. L. J. Zillman (Seattle, 1959), assembles a great mass of critical material. Of the many books on Shelley that include more or less on the drama, some are those of Carl Grabo (Chapel Hill, 1930 f.), F. Stovall (Durham, N.C., 1931), E. Barnard (Minneapolis, 1936), J. Barrell (New Haven, 1947), Carlos Baker (Princeton, 1948), J. A. Notopoulos (1949), P. H. Butter (Edinburgh, 1954), H. Bloom (New Haven, 1959), M. Wilson (New York, 1959), Hélène Lemaitre (Paris, 1962), R. G. Woodman (Toronto, 1964); and sections of the books by D. Bush (1937), D. Perkins (1959), H. Bloom (1961), and J. Benziger (1962), cited below in the Bibliography, II. Some studies of the drama alone are: K. N. Cameron, *PMLA* 58 (1943): pp. 728-753, on political symbolism; B. Weaver *(PMLA* 64, 1949, pp. 115-133) and J. R. Hurt *(Keats-Shelley Journal* 15, 1966, pp. 43-48) on Aeschylus and Shelley; R. H. Fogle, *Keats-Shelley Journal* 1 (1952): pp. 23-36; B. Weaver, *Prometheus Unbound* (Ann Arbor, 1957); E. R. Wasserman, *Shelley's Prometheus Unbound* (Baltimore, 1965). This last is an acute exegesis of metaphysical idealism which elucidates some difficulties and perhaps creates some: for instance, if Prometheus is the One Mind, "absolute being," "eternal and immutable," how does he undergo a radical change of heart? The latest and fullest explication of *Prometheus* is that of Seymour Reiter in his *Study of Shelley's Poetry* (University of New Mexico, 1967).

not grasp, or at any rate would not accept, Aeschylus' ultimate reconciling of Zeus and Prometheus; he also disavowed Milton's treatment of God and Satan. His Prometheus is a wholly righteous and heroic rebel against human and supposedly divine tyranny; he is above Satan in his selfless purity of motive and aim. In disowning his initial vengefulness, early in the first act, and in becoming filled with all-embracing love, Prometheus is set up as a Christ figure; and, like Shelley's perfect heroes in general, he can be sentimentalized.

In Aeschylus, if we take into our purview the lost parts of his trilogy, Zeus, the new, insecure, and hence cruel tyrant, eventually learns wisdom and maganimity, and Prometheus, the truculent friend of man, learns moderation and respect for law. In Shelley's widely different conception the abstract theme is too complex for the simple mythic plot, since both Prometheus and Jupiter represent man; the former, ideal imaginative man, the latter, the kinds of evil tyranny that man and man-made religion have established. This double projection of man's capacities for both good and evil, whatever its psychological and historical truth, causes some difficulties, and these may be aggravated by shifts between inward, individual conflict and mythic or objective and social terms. However, there remains a central resemblance to Aeschylus in the idea of regeneration as well as rebellion; the essential action in both dramas is mental. It is quite natural, therefore, that, as Shelley said in his preface, much of his imagery is "drawn from the operations of the human mind, or from those external actions by which they are expressed." But whereas Aeschylus builds up a unified conflict to a grand catastrophe, Shelley, after the first act, renders mental states with such figurative lavishness that drama largely evaporates and the thematic pattern is often clouded and weakened. Thus the overthrow of Jupiter is really accomplished when the power of love asserts itself in the soul of Prometheus, and the later dethronement of the tyrant becomes, whether dramatically or psychologically, a grotesque anticlimax.

The Renaissance poets, like the ancients, looked back to a golden age which had given way to human corruption, and they saw very limited possibilities of earthly amelioration for fallen man. But Bacon, one of Shelley's heroes, and later perfectibilitarian thinkers and the French Revolution effected a momentous change in the human outlook by transferring the golden age from a mythic past to a not unattainable future— and at the same time considerably altering the meaning of the idea. *Prometheus Unbound*, on its most obvious public level, is Shelley's most elaborate vision of that millennium that always hovered before him until near the end of his short life. And if his earliest polestar was William Godwin and his last Plato, this drama is an intensely Shelleyan blend of those not altogether harmonious elements. On the one hand we have the old Godwinian program (III.iv.130-204): the abolition of priests, kings, marriage, and other burdens will leave men and women "free from guilt or pain," "Equal, unclassed, tribeless, and nationless, / Exempt from awe. . . ." (This last phrase, which refers apparently to both religion and social classes, was used by Chapman, the Christian humanist, of runaway horses.)[28] On the other hand, "Platonic" is a vague word for the radiant visions of the ideal life and love and art to be achieved by the liberated creative imagination and for Shelley's pervasive sense of the world of existence as only a dark veil hiding the true reality. In the first act relatively concrete pictures of evil torture Prometheus, but thereafter soaring idealism may be prettified or fortified by idyllic or scientific images. The idyllic effects are heightened by the characteristically Shelleyan cluster of female figures: Asia, who appears to represent Aphrodite Urania, "Intellectual Beauty," Nature; and Panthea and Ione, whose symbolic roles remain debatable. In contrast with the strong, stark texture of Aeschylus, Shelley's prodigal mixture of image and idea can be both lush and obscurely subtle. At

---

[28]Chapman, *Hymne to Apollo,* line 370 *(Chapman's Homer,* ed. A. Nicoll (New York, 1956) , 2: p. 525) .

moments, however, his impassioned dreams give place to recognition of grim actuality, as in the lines of plain statement (I.625 f.) which Yeats echoed in *The Second Coming*:

> The good want power, but to weep barren tears.
> The powerful goodness want: worse need for them.
> The wise want love; and those who love want wisdom;
> And all best things are thus confused to ill.

In the almost entirely lyrical fourth act, an afterthought, the Spirits of the Hours and the Human Mind, of the Earth and the Moon, sing the rebirth of creative man in the millennial world of love and freedom. The Baconian Shelley rejoices too in scientific control of the forces of nature. In the song of Earth (370 f.) the picture of perfected man and perfect happiness—compared, say, with the choric ode on human powers in *Antigone* (332 f.) or with the ending of *Paradise Lost*—might to earlier ages have suggested the Greek sin of *hybris* or the Christian sin of pride. At the very end of the drama, however, after the prolonged, exultant vision of the golden age to come, Demogorgon admits the possible reappearance of evil, which must again be conquered by such virtues as Prometheus has displayed—although, set against the visionary idealism that animates most of the work, this and earlier glimpses of evil may seem only clouds on the edge of the rainbow. A partly similar emotional curve, one might add, was to appear in the last chorus of Shelley's *Hellas* ("The world's great age begins anew"), a triumphant imitation of Virgil's Messianic eclogue which ends in bitter disenchantment.

No poet shows so clearly as Keats the active presence of classical myth in the air, since even as a boy, reading where his own interest and his mentor, Charles Cowden Clarke, led him, he devoured the rather dusty handbooks we noticed before—and Leigh Hunt in his boyhood had devoured them too. Keats's response to myth was enriched, as he grew up, by his reading of Spenser, Shakespeare, Milton, and lesser poets, and by the vivifying imagination of such older contemporaries as Wordsworth,

Hunt, and Hazlitt.[29] There was nothing merely bookish or factitious in Keats's absorbing classical myth as a kind of native language; from the beginning it was interwoven with his intense delight in all the beauties of nature, from fields and flowers and streams to the sun and moon. For him the common sights of Hampstead Heath could suggest how poets had first conceived of fauns and dryads, of Psyche and Pan and Narcissus and Endymion.

While subjectivity is one of the textbook headings for Romanticism, in contrast with the neoclassical ideal of the public and impersonal, it must be qualified in regard to the poetry of myth. However individual the poet's idea or vision, his use of myth at once translates that idea or vision into more or less impersonal and universal terms—as it had done for Spenser and Milton. Most of Keats's major poems and some minor ones are concerned with an acutely personal problem, the nature and function of modern poetry and the modern poet. This might seem to mean a fatal narrowing of the scope of poetry and a narrowing of Keats's own audience to fellow poets; but of course his poems—and letters—have appealed strongly to multitudes of readers. The basic reason for the apparent paradox is that Keats's aesthetic and ethical ideas are not highbrow

---

[29]Some sources of Keats's mythology are noted in the *Poems*, ed. E. de Selincourt (5th ed., London, 1926), and in *John Keats: Selected Poems and Letters*, ed. D. Bush (Boston, 1959). All the critical books of course deal more or less with the mythological poems, e.g.: Margaret Sherwood, "Keats's Imaginative Approach to Myth," *Undercurrents of Influence in English Romantic Poetry* (Cambridge, Mass., 1934), pp. 203-264; C. L. Finney, *The Evolution of Keats's Poetry* (2 v., Cambridge, Mass., 1936); D. Bush, *Romantic Tradition* (Bibliography, II, below); Newell F. Ford, *The Prefigurative Imagination of John Keats: A Study of the Beauty-Truth Identification and Its Implications* (Stanford, 1951); J. M. Murry, *Keats* (London, 1955; enlarged from *Studies*, 1930 f.); E. C. Pettet, *On the Poetry of Keats* (Cambridge, 1957); D. Perkins and J. Benziger (below, Bibliography, II); the large critical biographies of W. J. Bate (Cambridge, Mass., 1963), Aileen Ward (New York, 1963), and Robert Gittings (London and Boston, 1968)—the first deals most fully with the poetry—and the small one by D. Bush (New York, 1966); Ian Jack (n. 9 above); W. H. Evert, *Aesthetic and Myth in the Poetry of Keats* (Princeton, 1965). Three special studies are: S. H. Larrabee (below, Bibliography, II), Ian Jack, *Keats and the Mirror of Art* (Oxford, 1967), and M. A. Goldberg, "John Keats and the Elgin Marbles," *Apollo* 82 (1965): pp. 370-377. Because of its intrinsic interest and because this book cannot go into Continental poetry, I must mention Paul de Man's "Keats and Hölderlin," *CL* 8 (1956-1957): pp. 28-45.

and esoteric but are rather those of the natural man whose faculties are only heightened in intensity. A supplementary reason is his use of classical myth, by which his convictions and questionings are distanced and broadened. Thus *Endymion* and the two *Hyperions* are both private and public poems.

One main problem with which Keats wrestled in verse and prose was whether it was enough for poetry to give sensuous pleasure or whether it should follow Wordsworth—and above all Shakespeare—and deal with "the agonies, the strife / Of human hearts." Keats's native endowment seemed, initially at least, to endorse the first alternative, his conscience and maturing ambitions drove him to the second. And there were various related problems. Does "beauty" mean an abstract principle, or beautiful things that perish? Does it embrace pain as well as pleasure? Are the senses sufficient in themselves, or are they the agents of intuitions that "burst our mortal bars," or must the poet possess intellectual knowledge? The ideal artist is surely an open-minded, impersonal creative power, like Shakespeare, not a doctrinaire prophet like Milton or Wordsworth or Shelley; yet can one be a serious poet unless through trouble and suffering he develops an ethical character? Finally, to go no further, there were times when Keats, with all his consuming dreams of poetic achievement, could set any and all kinds of poetry below personal integrity and humanitarian action.

Whether or not Keats had read Drayton's "Platonic" *Endimion and Phoebe*, he used the same plot in his own *Endymion*:[30] the poet-hero is won away from devotion to the moon-goddess by a supposed nymph or mortal who turns out to be the goddess in disguise. This plot Keats elaborated with so much wayward invention that his fable is sometimes obscured and has indeed been denied by a few critics who see nothing beyond

---

30Along with such general books as are cited in n. 29 above, some of the more recent studies of *Endymion* are: J. D. Wigod, *PMLA* 68 (1953): pp. 779-790; G. O. Allen, *Keats-Shelley Journal* 6 (1957): pp. 37-57; A. Gérard, *UTQ* 28 (1958-1959): pp. 160-175; S. M. Sperry, *Studies in Romanticism* (Boston University) 2 (1962): pp. 38-53; B. E. Miller, *Keats-Shelley Journal* 14 (1965): pp. 33-54; M. L. D'Avanzo, *Keats's Metaphors for the Poetic Imagination* (Durham, N.C., 1967), *passim*.

a celebration of sexual love. The orthodox view is that Endymion's quest of his goddess leads him through an ascending scale of experiences which culminate in humanitarian service and finally in the realization that his earthly love is the goddess he has sought. To philosophize this conclusion: the poet cannot achieve direct apprehension of an abstract ideal, but he may approach it through immediate experience of the concrete and particular. Such an idea is characteristically Keatsian and quite different from that of Shelley's earlier *Alastor*, in which the solitary poet-hero's failure to attain his ideal ends in death.

But the solution of *Endymion* was rather a wishful contrivance than an experienced revelation, and a year later, as Keats watched by the bedside of his dying brother, he again took up the problem, in *Hyperion*[31]—now with an immeasurable advance in poetic power due in part to study of *Paradise Lost*. At the council of the fallen Titans Oceanus explains their overthrow by the law of evolution: however beneficent their rule has been, they must give way to the more beautiful gods. Although Keats was in politics a thoughtful liberal, this general and aesthetic expression of faith in progress is in marked contrast with the explicit radicalism of the exactly contemporary *Prometheus Unbound*; we might think also of the Christian Spenser's use of the Titans and gods in the *Cantos of Mutability*. But apparently Oceanus' wisdom was intended to be seen as limited and implying an inadequate conception of beauty. Some months later, perhaps, just before he gave up the poem, Keats managed to get his central theme stated. Apollo—here, like Endymion, the archetypal poet—who has been oppressed by aching ignorance, undergoes a convulsive rebirth; he dies into life, becomes a god—that is, a true poet—

---

[31]Along with discussions of *Hyperion* and the *Fall* in the general books (n. 29 above), some special studies are: D. G. James (below, Bibliography, II) ; K. Muir, *Essays in Criticism* 2 (1952) : pp. 54-75, repr. in *John Keats: A Reassessment*, ed. K. Muir (Liverpool, 1958) ; J. D. Rosenberg, *Keats-Shelley Journal* 6 (1957) : pp. 87-95; B. Wicker, *Essays in Criticism* 7 (1957) : pp. 28-41; B. Blackstone, *The Consecrated Urn* (London, 1959), pp. 227-265; S. M. Sperry, *PMLA* 77 (1962) : pp. 77-84; E. E. Bostetter, *The Romantic Ventriloquists* (Seattle, 1963), pp. 136-180; K. Kroeber, *The Artifice of Reality* (Madison, 1964), pp. 137-153; R. D. Wagner, *Keats-Shelley Journal* 13 (1964) : pp. 29-41; Brian Wilkie, *Romantic Poets and Epic Tradition* (Madison, 1965), pp. 145-187.

when his mind is flooded with sympathetic knowledge of human suffering, of the troubled course of history. In Yeats's phrase, "A terrible beauty is born."[32] And we may observe that Keats's idea holds not merely for articulate poets but for all men who think and feel.

In April, 1819, perhaps soon after he added this unfinished conclusion, Keats wrote the first of his great odes, the *Ode to Psyche*. Imagining himself the priest of a goddess who had not received the worship accorded the early divinities of actual myth, Keats set forth what seems to be his conception of poetry in oblique and mainly luscious metaphors. While his ideas and moods often fluctuated, it appears strange to me—although notable critics see no weakness in the ode—that Keats, who had lately expressed through Apollo the poet's attaining of a tragic vision of life, could here relapse, at least in language and symbol, into what may be thought mere aesthetic reverie, like much of his early though far less beautiful verse. Even if, as some think, the theme of the ode is love, not poetry, one may still ask the question.

But the problem gnawed at him, and in the late summer he undertook to recast the epic *Hyperion* in the form of a vision. A new induction, Keats's last testament, is a symbolic parable which becomes painfully explicit in a dialogue between the poet-narrator and the Titaness Moneta, between, we might say, Keats's younger and his maturer self. Men are classified in successively narrowing divisions. First the selfish and thoughtless are distinguished from

> those to whom the miseries of the world
> Are misery, and will not let them rest.

Then there is a division between selfless, active servants of humanity and the tribe of poets, visionaries whose dreams poison their own and others' lives. Finally the poet of feverish egotistical dreams is distinguished from the true poet, who

> is a sage;
> A humanist, physician to all men.

---

[32] W. B. Yeats, *Easter 1916 (Collected Poems* (New York, Macmillan, 1965), p. 178).

But the climax comes when the narrator sees in Moneta's face a revelation akin to that of Apollo, of the poet of tragic vision who shares all human suffering. Though much has been said or implied about service of mankind, Keats's final emphasis is rather on insight and acceptance than, like Shelley's, on humanitarian love and progress.

Our two Victorian poets, Tennyson and Arnold, did not use classical myth in works on the scale of Shelley's and Keats's; but the shorter poems that concern us, dramatic monologues and reflective pieces (and the lyrics of *Empedocles on Etna*) similarly combine outward objectivity with personal feelings about mainly personal experience and questionings. Those questionings are both old and new.

Tennyson, because of his sensuous opulence, was early linked with Keats, though his early preoccupation with similar problems was apparently due, not to Keats's influence, but to Tennyson's breathing similar air and feeling similar pressures.[33] The poem *Timbuctoo*, which won a Cambridge medal in 1829, expressed the fear that modern science would wither "the great

---

[33]Four general studies are: a section in E. D. H. Johnson, *The Alien Vision of Victorian Poetry* (Princeton, 1952); J. H. Buckley, *Tennyson: The Growth of a Poet* (Cambridge, Mass., 1960); Valerie Pitt, *Tennyson Laureate* (London, 1962); and Elton E. Smith, *The Two Voices* (Lincoln, Neb., 1964). D. Bush (Bibliography, II, below) has a chapter on the mythological poems. On Arthur Hallam's early aesthetic phase, which Tennyson had shared, see below, III, n. 19, and pp. 665-666 in Joyce Green, "Tennyson's Development during the 'Ten Years' Silence' (1832-1842)," *PMLA* 66 (1951): pp. 662-697.

Some studies of individual poems are:

The Hesperides: G. R. Stange, *PMLA* 67 (1952): pp. 732-743, repr. in *Critical Essays on the Poetry of Tennyson,* ed. J. Killham (London, 1960); J. Adler, *Scripta Hierosolymitana* (Jerusalem, Hebrew University) 17 (1966): pp. 190-208.

The Lotos-Eaters: C. de L. Ryals, *Revue des Langues Vivantes* 25 (1959): pp. 474-486; M. MacLaren, *Classical Journal* 56 (1961): pp. 259-267; B. DeMott, *Kenyon Review* 24 (1962): pp. 442-456; A. Grob, *MP* 62 (1964-1965): pp. 118-129.

Œnone: P. Turner, *JEGP* 61 (1962): pp. 57-72, on echoes of the classics in relation to the whole poem.

The Palace of Art: W. Cadbury, *Criticism* 7 (1965): pp. 23-44; A. A. Mendilow, *Scripta* (see Adler, under *The Hesperides*) 17 (1966): pp. 155-189; J. Sendry, *Victorian Poetry* 4 (1966): pp. 149-162.

Ulysses. Along with the general books cited above, and some pages in W. B. Stanford (Bibliography, General, below) and R. Langbaum, *The Poetry of Experience* (New York, 1957), my file, doubtless far from complete, lists twenty-

Continued on page 51

vine of Fable"—or "myth," as we would say—which nourishes
man's essential life. In a number of early poems, some of them
mythological, Tennyson posed the question of the poet's
aesthetic detachment or social involvement. In one piece, *The
Poet* (1830), the poet is seen as the acknowledged legislator of
the world; but *The Poet's Mind*, of the same year, and other
poems of 1832 take a more or less opposite line. *The Hesperides* is a unique item in the canon, a magical and cryptic incantation in which the whole meaning is conveyed in allusive
symbols: the golden apples, the precious treasures of art, must
be guarded in their seclusion from Hercules, the outer world
of aggressive action. So too the Lady of Shalott, the cloistered
artist, dies when she encounters the outside world. In *The
Lotos-Eaters* Homeric folklore is reinterpreted in modern terms,
as Tennyson later said the old myths must be. Here alternate

---

odd articles on this poem. Some recent ones are: two in Killham (see *The
Hesperides* above); E. H. Duncan, *Tennessee Studies In Literature* 4 (1959):
pp. 13-30, largely on *Ulysses;* G. Roppen, *English Studies* 40 (1959): pp. 77-90,
and, with R. Sommers, *Strangers and Pilgrims* (Norwegian Studies in English
11 and New York, 1964); J. Pettigrew, *Victorian Poetry* 1 (1963): pp. 27-45;
C. Mitchell, *ibid.* 2 (1964): pp. 87-95; H. W. Fulweiler, *ibid.* 3 (1965): pp.
25-44, partly on *Ulysses;* and G. Pitts, *Philological Papers* (West Virginia
University) 15 (1966): pp. 36-42. Some of the recent critics, following, e.g.,
P. F. Baum *(Tennyson Sixty Years After,* Chapel Hill, 1948, pp. 299-303) and
E. D. H. Johnson, take Ulysses' voyage as an evasion of responsibility; Johnson
(Alien Vision, p. 41) sees Ulysses' resolve as merely the active counterpart of
the Lotos-Eaters' "more passive self-obsession." Some critics see a quest of death
or discount the personal element in the poem in favor of the dramatic. I find
no reason to doubt the essential truth of Tennyson's later recollections of the
state of mind expressed in the poem, and, accordingly, find no real contra-
diction in Ulysses' putting a high individual and inward motive above a
public one.

 Tithonus. M. J. Donahue (Mrs. Richard Ellmann), *PMLA* **64** (1949): pp.
400-416, described Tennyson's revision. E. D. H. Johnson *(Alien Vision,* p. 13)
sees, along with the obvious theme, "almost certainly a symbolic representation
of Tennyson's aesthetic philosophy. Taken so, Eos stands for the Keatsian ideal
of beauty which holds the poet in bondage." I have strong doubts of this.

 Tiresias. With Tennyson's conclusion *cf.* Pindar (Loeb Classical Library, p.
591) and Pindar's second Olympian ode. Johnson (p. 67) sees the old prophet-
artist accepting his isolation with its burden of intuitions that he cannot share
with the outer world.

 Demeter and Persephone: G. R. Stange, *ELH* 21 (1954): pp. 67-80; pp. 25-28
in J. Kissane, "Victorian Mythology," *Victorian Studies* 6 (1962): pp. 5-28.
While Stange sees affinities with Frazer, Kissane (25) finds "a far richer
affinity" with Pater's "The Myth of Demeter and Persephone" (1876: repr. in
Greek Studies, 1895). E. D. H. Johnson (66) sees in the poem a new version
of Tennyson's old problem of outward involvement or withdrawal into the
creative depths of consciousness.

stanzas depict the languorous pleasures of irresponsible withdrawal from life and the barren pains of active participation: withdrawal is implicitly condemned, but the seductive images, language, and rhythms show how strongly Tennyson could feel the temptation. In *Œnone,* Paris chooses a beautiful wife, a private gratification, in preference to the career of moral wisdom and action offered by Pallas, and the choice proves disastrous. In the openly allegorical *Palace of Art* the eventual horrors of aesthetic isolation—which anticipate the later decadence—are countered, rather summarily, by penitent acceptance of life and the idea of shared culture.

So far, we might say, Tennyson's concern with this problem, however serious, had been in the domain of theory; but the shock of Arthur Hallam's death gave it a new depth and a partly new focus. In *The Two Voices* Tennyson arrived at affirmation only after a prolonged struggle with suicidal nihilism, and these two voices spoke separately in two of his finest classical poems, *Ulysses* and *Tithonus.* Since both monologues are supposedly uttered by old men, we may remember that the poet was only twenty-four (*Tithonus* was revised and finished later). Although *Ulysses* has Homeric echoes, the main conception, as everyone knows, comes from Dante (*Inferno* xxvi). But whereas Dante had taken Ulysses' westward voyage as a manifestation of sinful curiosity and pride, for Tennyson the quest of experience and knowledge is a grand Romantic, half-Faustian enterprise and, in a more personal way, an inspiring example of heroic resolution. Here the dilemma of earlier poems is somewhat complicated, because Ulysses' voyage can be said to represent avoidance as well as acceptance of responsibility. Yet the whole force of the poem is on the positive side and accords with Tennyson's later statement, made with reference to *In Memoriam:* "There is more about myself in 'Ulysses,' which was written under the sense of loss and that all had gone by, but that still life must be fought out to the end. It was more written with the feeling of his loss upon me than many poems in 'In Memoriam.' "[34]

---

[34]Sir James Knowles, "Aspects of Tennyson," *Nineteenth Century* 33 (1893): p. 182; quoted in D. Bush, *Romantic Tradition,* p. 209.

Apart from the Homeric setting, Ulysses is a real man in a real world, the nineteenth-century world, but Tithonus is a mythic, half-ghostly figure who addresses Eos in language that applies at once to the goddess and the cosmic phenomenon of the dawn. If *Ulysses* expressed Tennyson's conviction of "the need of going forward, and braving the struggle of life,"[35] *Tithonus* was a vain plea for release from the burden of living. (Some critics see a death-wish in *Ulysses* also, but I do not.) While Ulysses—with some significant echoes of *Hamlet*[36]—cannot endure the gross routine of ordinary men and seeks a new strange world of experience, Tithonus, doomed to "cruel immortality," longs for the common fate of mankind. Both poems grow out of the same complex of feelings as *In Memoriam*, but both exclude any direct concern with religious faith: the poet who clung so passionately to belief in immortality has Tithonus crave extinction and Ulysses refer to "that eternal silence"—though he may "touch the Happy Isles, / And see the great Achilles, whom we knew," that is, the dead Hallam. These two poems, whose contradictory moods were quite natural in Tennyson's situation, remind us that, for him and other poets, the dramatic monologue allowed the impersonal expression of a free range of ideas.[37]

Tiresias, written partly at the time of *Ulysses* but completed much later, belongs in spirit to the poet's old age. The Theban prophet, like Tennyson, had had "some strange hope to see the nearer God," and, like Tennyson, he recoils from a world of growing violence and corruption; he longs for release from life and translation to the Isles of the Blest. When Tennyson in direct terms assailed his age or expressed a vague faith in some far-off amelioration, he was likely to be either journalistic or pietistic; but here, embellishing a fragment of Pindar, he achieves elegiac splendor in a picture of the otherworld of

---

[35]Hallam Lord Tennyson, *Alfred Lord Tennyson: A Memoir* (2 v., New York, 1897) , 1, p. 496.

[36]Compare *Ulysses*, lines 5 and 22-24, with *Hamlet* IV. iv. 32 f., lines uttered by Hamlet after he has seen Fortinbras go by. Tennyson seems closer to this than to lines that his have been linked with, *Troilus and Cressida* III. iii. 150 153. (D. Bush, *MLR* 38, 1943, p. 38) .

[37]See especially R. Langbaum (n. 33 above, under *Ulysses*).

visible gods and heroes and heroic harmony of hearts and deeds and worship.

One of the last great products of Tennyson's astonishing vitality, *Demeter and Persephone*, written when he was seventy-seven, is at once a public poem and an old man's testament. In mythic conception and manner it goes beyond the simpler *Tithonus*. The meeting of Demeter and the daughter she had sought throughout the world, the daughter who is now queen of Hades, involves the continual juxtaposition of darkness and light, death and rebirth, despair and hope. The hope for mankind, for "younger kindlier Gods," recalls the speech of Keats's Oceanus—or various non-mythological and weaker utterances of Tennyson's—but the whole theme is presented through allusive images which fill the poem with a sense of the mystery and pain that envelop life. Tennyson's use here, as in his earlier mythological poems, of the dramatic monologue ensured a consistently secular and pagan texture and tone, though we might have expected his religious concern to show through the mask. And while all these poems except the last might perhaps be called poems of escape, the label would be unfair because the poet's idealism includes sober recognition of actuality.

From this late poem of Tennyson we go back a generation to look at one more poet, the young Matthew Arnold.[38] As artist and imaginative creator Arnold rarely approached Tenny-

---

[38]For Arnold's poetry critical aids of diverse size and focus are: Lionel Trilling, *Matthew Arnold* (New York, 1939) ; C. B. Tinker and H. F. Lowry, *The Poetry of Matthew Arnold: A Commentary* (New York, 1940) ; Louis Bonnerot, *Matthew Arnold Poète: Essai de biographie psychologique* (Paris, 1947) ; E. D. H. Johnson, *The Alien Vision* (see n. 33 above) ; Paull F. Baum, *Ten Studies in the Poetry of Matthew Arnold* (Durham, N.C., 1958) ; W. Stacy Johnson, *The Voices of Matthew Arnold* (New Haven, 1961) ; Warren D. Anderson, *Matthew Arnold and the Classical Tradition* (Ann Arbor, 1965) ; A. Dwight Culler, *Imaginative Reason: The Poetry of Matthew Arnold* (New Haven, 1966) ; G. R. Stange, *Matthew Arnold: The Poet as Humanist* (Princeton, 1967) ; and the valuable apparatus in *The Poems of Matthew Arnold*, ed. K. Allott (London, 1965). Among the many short studies are sections in D. Bush, *Romantic Tradition* (Bibliography, II, below) ; George H. Ford, *Keats and the Victorians* (New Haven, 1944) , and J. Hillis Miller, *The Disappearance of God* (Cambridge, Mass., 1963) ; and discussions of *Empedocles* by F. Kermode *(Romantic Image* (London, 1957)) and W. E. Houghton *(Victorian Studies* 1 (1957-1958) : pp. 311-336). Arnold's state of mind during his most poetical years is best revealed—apart from the poems—in *The Letters of Matthew Arnold to Arthur Hugh Clough*, ed. H. F. Lowry (New York, 1932) .

son or Keats, but he approaches modern poets in his deep and analytical awareness of his own and the age's *malaise*. Placed in an ugly, busy, confused, and confusing world, Arnold seeks above all things to possess his own soul, to achieve integrity and totality of being. The sense of oneness with nature, which had more or less sustained Coleridge and Wordsworth, is no longer possible: man is alone, alone in a world that seems to have no meaning. Craving direction, Arnold imposes on himself the rigorous discipline of Stoic reason; yet that tends to cramp and deaden what may be a better guide, the spontaneous, instinctive feeling of youth, love, fullness of life. Thus Arnold's self-searching poetry is a network of unresolved tensions, and some of these are reflected in his use of myth.

The title poem of his first volume, *The Strayed Reveller* (1849), recalls Keats and the early Tennyson in dealing with poetry and the poet.[39] A young follower of Dionysus, encountering Circe and Ulysses, the man of action, drinks of Circe's here innocuous potion and is enabled to see, like the remote, untroubled gods, the varied spectacle of mortal life. But the poet does not have the serene detachment of the gods; he cannot sing unless he has imaginative experience of human ills, a tragic vision. *Philomela,* a lyrical statement of that kind of vision, has a fitting place between Keats's *Ode to a Nightingale* and T. S. Eliot's allusions: the bird's song, heard in England in the cool moonlight, bridges time and space as a symbol, for all its beauty, of "Eternal passion! Eternal pain!" *Philomela* rehearses, allusively, the original myth; *The New Sirens,* like a number of modern poems, is mythological chiefly in the implications of its title. Whereas the Homeric Sirens, offering knowledge, lured men to destruction, the new sirens offer romantic passion as high fulfillment; but that, the poet

---

39L. A. Gottfried *(RES* 11 (1960) : pp. 403-409) suggested that Arnold's "strayed reveller" was partly modeled on Keats. However remote such an idea is from our view of Keats, or from Arnold's own later view, it is no doubt possible (though Arnold even at this time recognized Keats's "very high gift"), since Keats was so commonly regarded as a voluptuary of sensation and since Arnold spoke of his (and Browning's) reflecting "the world's multitudinousness" and of his (and Shelley's) reviving of Elizabethan luxuriance *(Letters,* ed. Lowry, pp. 97, 124). We may remember that at this time (1848-1852) *The Fall of Hyperion* had not yet been printed.

knows, means only half-spurious ecstasy and then ennui.[40] Arnold discounts in advance the neopagan raptures and languors of the young Swinburne—who, by the way, admired the poem.[41]

Other poems are more openly and pointedly ethical. In the non-mythological *Mycerinus* the exemplary young king, whose father had flourished long in iniquity, is doomed to an early death, and he turns away bitterly from religion and philosophy to give his few remaining years to sensual revelry. Arnold's response to unmerited calamity cannot be that of Job. The ambiguous conclusion suggests that Mycerinus attains understanding of virtue as its own and only reward. The later *Palladium* is wholly positive and forthright: the statue of Pallas, on which the safety of Troy depended, remains above the perpetual turmoil and confusion of life as a perpetual symbol of the inward strength of the soul—what the Arnold of prose, mindful of the old classical-Christian tradition of "right reason," called "our best self."[42]

But again and again the other side of Arnold appears in a nostalgic and vain desire for the beauty, simplicity, and power of pure feeling, the kind of feeling that was a sure guide in the Biblical and mythical childhood of the race, long

---

[40]Arnold supplied a prose "argument" for *The New Sirens* (*Letters,* ed. Lowry, pp. 105-106; *Poems,* ed. Allott, pp. 34-35). Allott cites the debate in chapters 33-38 of *Lélia,* by George Sand, whom the young Arnold so greatly admired. In the "argument," if not in the poem, the Greek Sirens are "the fierce sensual lovers of antiquity," a post-Homeric idea (W. D. Anderson, pp. 226-227, n. 12: see n. 38 above). The erotic temptation had appeared in the church fathers and Alexandrian allegorists (Hugo Rahner (Bibliography, General, below), pp. 328-386, especially pp. 354 f.) and in Fulgentius, *Fab.* ii. 8. W. B. Stanford (pp. 124-125: see below, Bibliography, General) cites, e.g., Cicero, *De Finibus* V. xviii. 49, where the temptation is knowledge, and, for the temptation of pleasure, Seneca, *Ep.* cxxiii. 12, lvi. 15, xxxi. 1-2.

[41]Swinburne, *Essays and Studies* (London, 1875), p. 125 (cited by Allott, p. 34).

[42]*Palladium* was perhaps written "not earlier than Sept. 1864" (*Poems,* ed. Allott, p. 494). Along with Arnold's devotion to Homer, and Allott's citations from E. Scherer and Lucretius (ii. 5-6), we may recall the remark of Goethe which Arnold quoted in *On Translating Homer* (1861): "From Homer and Polygnotus I every day learn more clearly that in our life here above ground we have, properly speaking, to enact Hell" (*Matthew Arnold: On the Classical Tradition,* ed. R. H. Super (Ann Arbor, 1960), p. 102). A very pertinent entry in the Yale Manuscript of Arnold is quoted by Tinker and Lowry (n. 38 above), p. 190, and by E. D. H. Johnson (*Alien Vision,* p. 157).

before the modern dialogue of the mind with itself. He has diverse symbols for this instinctive wholeness of heart: ancient Judea and Greece, his love for the mysterious Marguerite, the poetry of Wordsworth, the peace of nature ("the rural Pan" in contrast with "the city's jar"), the Scholar Gipsy for ever fleeing human contact and contagion. The "river of Time," most commonly an image of continuity, may also, seen as coming from a mountain source, stand for primitive purity and clarity of life and impulse. And some of Arnold's rivers flow into the sea of Neoplatonic infinity and eternity—a symbol drawn chiefly, no doubt, from Wordsworth's *Intimations of Immortality*.

The primitivism of Arnold the Stoic is rarely escapist. The conflict between deliberate, rational self-discipline and the buried life of feeling is almost a drawn battle in his major work, *Empedocles on Etna*. The restless, consuming intellect of the philosopher has burned out his capacity for simple feeling, for Wordsworthian joy. That capacity is embodied in the youthful singer Callicles, whose mythological lyrics are no mere interludes. In the first one the young Achilles learns from Chiron the centaur the simple creed of the heroic age; in the last, sung after the despairing Empedocles has plunged into the crater, Apollo and the Muses hymn the old verities and pieties of nature and faith. Empedocles and Callicles are the most elaborate projections of Arnold's opposed selves, and, though he knows that it is too late in history to be Callicles, it is the singer who is given the last word.[43] A variation on

---

43A. D. Culler, in his excellent book (p. 177: see n. 38 above), says that "the Apollo who leads the Muses is . . . a new type of poet who will announce, as the proper subjects of poetry, those set forth in the Preface of 1853. . . . 'actions; human actions. . . . Those . . . which most powerfully appeal to the great human affections. . . .'" M. B. Raymond ("Apollo and Arnold's 'Empedocles on Etna,'" *Review of English Literature* 8, 3 (1967): pp. 22-32) also sees Callicles, the representative of harmonious Apollonian art, as reinforcing Arnold's Preface, a view which, he says, supports Houghton (n. 38 above). But if *Empedocles* ends in agreement with the Preface, Arnold's reason for suppressing it would seem to be considerably weakened. I still think, as I thought long ago (*Romantic Tradition*, p. 258), that the final lyric reaffirms the simple—and for modern man inadequate—creed partly expressed in the first lyric, and that, while it may touch the principles of the Preface, it belongs more to Arnold's nostalgic primitivism than to his new and positive classicism. From the standpoint of Arnold the critic, Callicles, however genuine and attractive in his serene simplicity, would be like the English Romantic poets: he "did not know enough"—and Empedocles knew too much.

this conflict appears in the later *Thyrsis*: Arthur Hugh Clough, the close friend of Arnold's earlier years, the very type of the age's intellectual and spiritual distress, is seen against the pastoral simplicity of ancient Greece and the Oxford country-side of their youth.

When we think of our four mythological poets, Shelley and Keats, Tennyson and Arnold, we think at once of great differences among the four, between the two generations, and, in a still larger perspective, between all four and the poets of the Renaissance. These last had shared a universal sense of the stability of all things classical, an accepted body of serious mythological interpretation (to be modified within reason), a relatively unquestioned religious faith; and they had no or almost no difficulty in putting pagan myths and symbols to Christian as well as secular uses. Of course, in spite of such a partly happy situation, no one is likely to think of Spenser, Shakespeare, and Milton as facile optimists.

The Romantic revival of myth came after a period of rationalistic sterility or enlightenment (whichever word we prefer), and it partook of all the dynamic impulses that made the Romantic movement so comprehensive and so powerful. But, though we have taken account of many great poems, our central theme, pagan myth and Christian tradition, might be said to have almost disappeared,[44] because the two terms have lost their old active meaning and relationship. To Christianity Shelley of course was intensely hostile, though he came to revere Christ; Keats, who might be labeled a Deist, was, as poet, indifferent, though he had his own vision of life as a vale of soul-making. Tennyson and Arnold were at the center of the Victorian religious crisis and most of their chief poetry, including the mythological, is conditioned by that fact; but the poems we have looked at are all kept decorously classical and secular in tone, and religion, if present at all, remains in the background or between the lines. Obviously none of the four poets was a "neopagan."

---

[44]One late (and non-mythological) exception is the contrast drawn, in Arnold's *Obermann Once More*, between the hellish self-disgust of "that hard Pagan world" (with an example from Lucretius iii.1060-1067) and the new-born hope, and asceticism, of Christianity. See below, III, n. 35.

For the Victorians the failure of traditional religious belief was the main but not the only loss. Few poets could any longer feel either the spiritualized nature of the early Wordsworth or the mythologized or mythic nature of Keats or Shelley. For Tennyson nature was simply itself, ageless in beauty or in blind destructiveness, rich in images of human moods and destiny, but seldom a really mythic world of Olympian or terrestrial divinities; in that respect the younger Arnold was nearer to the Romantics. If orthodox religion was crumbling, and if nature was emptied of spiritual meaning, classical myth might seem to be a last symbolic medium for transcendental longings; but even these were subject to the general process of skeptical attrition—a process already epitomized in the poetry of Keats, indeed in his early *Endymion* alone. Thus poets, more or less alienated from accepted religious, political, and social creeds and attitudes, reinterpreted myths predominantly as vehicles for their own experience or vision or their own reflections on the problems of their age. One remarkable thing, from Keats up through Arnold, is the number of mythological poems, long and short, given to the special problems of the poet in the modern world—an index of mounting difficulties and mounting self-consciousness; yet many of these poems, as their continuing vitality attests, are, by extended implication, concerned with the problems of any thoughtful modern man.

Notwithstanding the number and quality of the poems we have reviewed, we might, if we had been living, say, about 1860, have made one more prediction that classical myth was at last really dead, that it could not survive through an age of advancing skepticism, science, and industrialism, an age in which some critics and poets were insisting on the necessity of modern subjects, in which the validity of poetry itself could be in doubt. But, although many later poets seem to have accepted, with or without regret, the death of the gods and heroes, many others have felt our civilization's emotional and imaginative need of myth. Some of the chief writers in English and other languages have shown that classical myth can still be fresh and powerful; and even the old pagan-Christian antinomy has been both revived and resolved.

III. The Modern Period

SINCE OUR MAIN concern here is with the twentieth century, we must skim over the latter half of the nineteenth. During that period the original strength and breadth and depth of Romanticism were attenuated by some leading poets and critics who more or less withdrew from the world into a palace of art or ivory tower. From an increasingly industrial, commercial, Philistine civilization there was no escape except through art; alienation became a very positive creed. The religion of art for art's sake, nourished from a variety of English and Continental sources, had as its successive high priests Rossetti, Walter Pater, and Oscar Wilde.[1] Pater and Wilde and others cherished some aestheticized notions of Greek culture which were more congenial than historical:[2] it might be unfair to say that it was all done with mirrors.

This movement had predictable effects in our special domain. The great theme of Troy, which had evoked major works from Chaucer and Shakespeare, dwindled for Rossetti into the decadent conception of Helen as a *femme fatale*. A similar Helen had already appeared in William Morris' early, unpublished *Scenes from the Fall of Troy*. These have their dramatic moments, but their romantic medievalism foreshadows

[1]Some references for the aesthetic movement (apart from books on individual writers) are: W. B. Yeats, *Autobiographies* (n. 19 below); T. Earle Welby, *The Victorian Romantics 1850-1870* (London, 1929); Albert J. Farmer, *Le Mouvement esthétique et "décadent" en Angleterre (1873-1900)* (Paris, 1931); Louise Rosenblatt, *L'Idée de l'art pour l'art dans la littérature anglaise pendant la période victorienne* (Paris, 1931); Sir B. Ifor Evans, *English Poetry in the Later Nineteenth Century* (London, 1933; rev. ed., 1966); William Gaunt, *The Pre-Raphaelite Tragedy* (London, 1942) and *The Aesthetic Adventure* (London, 1945); Graham Hough (n. 7 below); Barbara Charlesworth, *Dark Passages: The Decadent Consciousness in Victorian Literature* (Madison, 1965); William E. Fredeman, *Pre-Raphaelitism: A Bibliocritical Study* (Cambridge, Mass., 1965).

[2]The Dionysian and Apollonian and other mythic strains in Pater's writings are elaborately studied in Gerald C. Monsman, *Pater's Portraits: Mythic Pattern in the Fiction of Walter Pater* (Baltimore, 1967).

the long and dreamily stylized narratives, *The Life and Death of Jason* (1867) and the classical myths of *The Earthly Paradise* (1868 f.), hypnotic poems of escape from London and "six counties overhung with smoke." Ancient Greece is not here the nursery of allegorical and ethical mythology or of political liberty but a never-never land of the senses, of beauty, love, and death.[3] We should not, though, forget that Morris became an active Socialist—or that Swinburne was to celebrate the Italian struggle for freedom.

Swinburne was compounded of diverse elements, from a Hellenism both authentic and decadent to a sadism (and masochism) authenticated by knowledge of De Sade. These strains, and others, appeared in his early drama, *Atalanta in Calydon* (1865):[4] Meleager, the hero of the boar hunt, becomes a helpless victim of love, his mother, and the gods. The "pagan" implications of the drama would have been clear enough even if the young poet had not devoted a chorus to denunciation of "the supreme evil, God." (Tennyson asked him whether it was fair to use the style of the Hebrew prophets for that purpose.[5]) But, for those who could stomach such sentiments, there was what Tennyson called the "strength and splendour" of the poetry, both the billowing choruses and the majestic blank verse. For most modern readers—one exception is the late E. E. Cummings[6]—the intoxicating magic has so far faded

[3]*Scenes from the Fall of Troy* were first printed in Morris' *Collected Works,* ed. May Morris, 24 (London, 1915). His mythological poems are discussed by D. Bush, *Romantic Tradition,* pp. 297-327; Oscar Maurer, "William Morris and the Poetry of Escape," *Nineteenth-Century Studies,* ed. Herbert Davis *et al.* (Ithaca, 1940), pp. 247-276, and "Morris's Treatment of Greek Legend in *The Earthly Paradise,*" *Studies in English* (University of Texas, 1954), 33: pp. 103-118; Paul Thompson, *The Work of William Morris* (London, 1967), pp. 170-180.

[4]The fullest study of Swinburne's mythological poems and plays is William R. Rutland, *Swinburne: A Nineteenth Century Hellene* (Oxford, 1931). See also D. Bush, *Romantic Tradition,* pp. 328-357, and references; R. Del Re, "Il classicismo nella poesia di . . . Swinburne dagli studi dell'adolescenza all' 'Atalanta,' " *Convivium* 28, N.S. (1960): pp. 20-44, 165-179.

[5]Hallam Lord Tennyson, *Alfred Lord Tennyson: A Memoir* (2 v., New York, 1897) 1, p. 496. See H. A. Hargreaves, "Swinburne's Greek Plays and God, 'The Supreme Evil,' " *MLN* 76 (1961): pp. 607-616.

[6]Cummings, who read some of his favorite poems along with his Norton lectures at Harvard, delivered with unspoiled gusto the first chorus of *Atalanta* (*Six NonLectures,* Cambridge, Mass., 1953, pp. 38-39).

that *Atalanta* may seem to be only "literature," a wax model, though it has been held that Swinburne's shimmering images and texture, in his poetry at large, anticipated Symbolist effects.

In the next year, 1866, Swinburne's *Poems and Ballads* thrust upon the English public some of those picturesque and pathological themes and attitudes that Mario Praz has described under the title *The Romantic Agony*. Along with much that was novel, motifs which had appeared in Tennyson and Arnold —as in *The Lotos-Eaters* and *The Palace of Art* and *Tithonus* and *The New Sirens*—now assumed a dark and diabolical hue as the un-English phenomena of decadence: the ecstasies and torments of normal or abnormal passion, sensual delight in pain endured or inflicted, immense ennui, a loathing for life and longing for death. One *locus classicus* of Swinburnian neopaganism was the *Hymn to Proserpine (after the Proclamation in Rome of the Christian Faith):*

> Wilt thou yet take all, Galilean? but these thou shalt not take,
> The laurel, the palms and the pæan, the breasts of the nymphs
>   in the brake. . . .
> Thou hast conquered, O pale Galilean; the world has grown
>   grey from thy breath;
> We have drunken of things Lethean, we have fed on the fullness
>   of death.[7]

This theme received further sentimental exploitation from sundry small poets such as Oscar Wilde, who, although so clever, was a fluent purveyor of all the fashionable clichés, both neopagan and Christian.[8]

One strain in this modern neopaganism must have a word more. We remember the diverse meanings attached to the god Pan by Renaissance mythographers and such poets as Spenser

---

[7]Graham Hough *(The Last Romantics* (London, 1949) , p. 190) quotes these lines as an echo of Gautier, whom Swinburne admired: "Des dieux que l'art toujours révère / Trônaient au ciel marmoréen; / Mais l'Olympe cède au Calvaire, / Jupiter au Nazaréen; / Une voix dit: Pan est mort!—L'ombre / S'étend" *(Bûchers et Tombeaux).*

[8]In the full and able study of Epifanio San Juan, *The Art of Oscar Wilde* (Princeton, 1967) , discussion of the poems (pp. 19-48) includes references to scholarship and criticism.

and Milton; we remember too the ancient tale of the voice proclaiming, at the time of the Crucifixion, that "Great Pan is dead." The nostalgic pagan raptures of Schiller's *Gods of Greece* inspired an impassioned reply, *The Dead Pan* (1844), from Mrs. Browning, whose Grecian fervor was second to her Christian faith (her husband was drawn rather to the shaggy goat-god).[9] In the later Victorian age Pan appeared as a symbol of natural, primitive instinct breaking loose from the unnatural conventions of polite society; in both old and New England many ladies and gentlemen sat in their studies and piped decorously of Pan and woodland freedom. Pan could, though, have more serious meaning for more important writers. E. M. Forster, who had assimilated the somewhat sentimental Hellenism of Pater and Lowes Dickinson, could set Pan (and modern Italians) in opposition to the artificial restraints of suburban gentility.[10] And Pan, with other divinities, had a more violent apostle of primitivism in D. H. Lawrence, who rebelled fiercely against the deadening effects of science and glorified "transfiguration through ecstasy in the flesh." "Knowledge" has killed the sun and moon, the machine has killed the earth.

> How . . . are we to get back the grand orbs of the soul's heavens, that fill us with unspeakable joy? How are we to get back Apollo, and Attis, Demeter, Persephone, and the halls of Dis? . . . . We've got to get them back, for they are the world our soul, our greater consciousness, lives in. The world of reason and science . . . is the dry and sterile little world the abstracted mind inhabits. . . . But the two ways of knowing, for man, are knowing in terms of apartness, which

---

[9] Mrs. Browning's *Dead Pan* is discussed by D. Bush, *Romantic Tradition*, p. 268, and by Patricia Merivale (below, Bibliography, III).

[10] For E. M. Forster, see W. R. Irwin and P. Merivale (below, Bibliography, III); F. C. Crews, "E. M. Forster: The Limitations of Mythology," *CL* 12 (1960): pp. 97-112; Alan Wilde, *Art and Order: A Study of E. M. Forster* (New York, 1964); Wilfred Stone, *The Cave and the Mountain: A Study of E. M. Forster* (Stanford, 1966).

To throw in a very different bit of information, Robert Payne's *The Great God Pan* (New York, 1952) is a life of Charles Chaplin.

is mental, rational, scientific, and knowing in terms of together-
ness, which is religious and poetic.[11]

Long before Lawrence, Nietzsche, who likewise saw the great
enemy of myth, and man, in scientific analysis, had declared:

> Yet every culture that has lost myth has lost, by the same
> token, its natural, healthy creativity. Only a horizon ringed
> about with myths can unify a culture. . . . Man today, stripped
> of myth, stands famished among all his pasts and must dig
> frantically for roots, be it among the most remote antiquities.[12]

However large the differences, these outbursts recall Coleridge's
protests against the mechanistic rationalism of the eighteenth
century, his nostalgia for classical myth, and his doctrine of
organicism: "we are all *one Life.*"[13] The whole situation is
suggested by a pregnant saying: that nature, in ceasing to be
divine, ceased to be human.[14]

It seems to be generally agreed among our urban intellec-
tuals that modern civilization has cut man off from the rhythms
of earth, starved his senses and imagination, and undertaken
to replace the individual personality with mass-produced robots
fed on mass-produced fantasy. Feelings of revolt can of course
be only a sentimental stereotype, but they can also be deeply

---

[11]D. H. Lawrence, *A Propos of Lady Chatterley's Lover* (London, Mandrake
Press, 1930), pp. 54-55; repr. in *Sex, Literature and Censorship*, ed. H. T.
Moore (New York, Twayne Publishers, 1953), pp. 117-118. Along with the
books on Lawrence, see, e.g., W. R. Irwin (below, Bibliography, III); J.
Kessler, "D. H. Lawrence's Primitivism," *Texas Studies in Literature and
Language* 5 (1963-1964): pp. 467-488; P. Merivale, "D. H. Lawrence and the
Modern Pan Myth," *ibid.* 6 (1964-1965): pp. 297-305, and her forthcoming book
on the history of the myth (below, Bibliography, General); G. A. Panichas,
"D. H. Lawrence and the Ancient Greeks," *English Miscellany* 16 (1965): pp.
195-214. One notable and relevant poem is *Bavarian Gentians* (*Complete Poems
of D. H. Lawrence*, ed. V. de S. Pinto and W. Roberts (2 v., New York, 1964)
2: p. 697. On the process of its composition see R. W. Harvey, *Wascana Review*
1 (1966): pp. 74-86.

[12]Friedrich Nietzsche, *The Birth of Tragedy and The Genealogy of Morals*,
tr. F. Golffing (New York, Doubleday, 1956), pp. 136-137. For a compendious
survey of Nietzsche and of ritualistic ideas of tragedy (Gilbert Murray, Herbert
Weisinger, *et al.*), see B. L. Reid, *William Butler Yeats* (n. 19 below), pp. 3-44.

[13]Coleridge, in a letter to Sotheby of September 10, 1802 (*Letters,* ed. E. L.
Griggs, 2 (Oxford, 1956): p. 864).

[14]I have met this saying attributed to John Dewey, but I have not found it
in his writings and it does not sound like him.

authentic. The necessity of myth and the mythic faculty got some support from Freud and much more from Jung's doctrine of the racial memory or collective unconscious—what Yeats, going back to the seventeenth-century Platonist Henry More, called the *Anima Mundi*.[15] And modern criticism has been preoccupied, in fruitful and other ways, with myth and symbol. As for mythology in our restricted sense, through most of the nineteenth century scholarly writing seems to have had much less influence on poetry than it had in earlier ages; at any rate poets did not follow Max Müller in seeing almost all Greek myths as solar. With the rise of a new tribe of classical scholars, Frazer, Jane Harrison, Gilbert Murray, and others, it looked as if Müller's myths of the sun were to be transferred wholesale to the Vegetation Spirit;[16] an archetypal pattern of death and rebirth was exemplified in the myths of Adonis, Attis, and Dionysus. The great modern bible of myth, *The Golden Bough*, began to appear in 1890, and Lionel Trilling affirms that "Perhaps no book has had so decisive an effect upon modern literature as Frazer's."[17] Obviously *The Golden Bough* far surpassed the works of earlier mythographers in learning. Obviously, too, it was remote from the medieval and

---

[15]Yeats, *Autobiographies* (New York, Macmillan, 1927), pp. 324, 328; *Per Amica Silentia Lunae*, in *Essays* (New York, Macmillan, 1924), pp. 511, 514 f.; and many of Yeats's critics, e.g., G. Melchiori (n. 19 below), pp. 26-32. Melchiori (p. 29) mistakenly credits Henry More with a book entitled *Anima Mundi*.

[16]R. M. Dorson, "The Eclipse of Solar Mythology" (below, Bibliography, III).

[17]Lionel Trilling, *Beyond Culture* (New York, Viking Press, 1965), p. 14. *Cf.* T. S. Eliot's notes on *The Waste Land*, and J. B. Vickery (below, Bibliography, III).

Michael Grant remarks: "Indeed, the revitalizing of the classical myths can be claimed as the most significant of all the impacts that the Graeco-Roman world has made upon modern thought" (*Myths of the Greeks and Romans* (London, Weidenfeld and Nicolson, 1962), p. xx).

Alex Zwerdling (*PMLA* 79 (1964): pp. 447-456: below, Bibliography, II) sees the objective view of mythology as inaugurated by Lempriere (1788 f.), *Bell's New Pantheon* (1790), William Godwin's *The Pantheon* (1806), and Richard Payne Knight's *Inquiry into the Symbolical Language of Ancient Art and Mythology* (1818), and, with more modern, scientific sophistication, by the Germans Karl Otfried Müller (1825) and C. A. Lobeck. J. Kissane ("Victorian Mythology": below, Bibliography, III) describes as "humanistic" rather than "anthropological" the views of Ruskin, Pater, and J. A. Symonds especially.

Renaissance books that found in myth ethical *exempla* or refractions of Biblical truth; Frazer's work was rather in the skeptical tradition and tended to reduce Christianity to mythic fiction.

Before we come to our chief modern poets we may recall the poetical scene in the period 1880-1914 from which they emerged. The early Pre-Raphaelite and aesthetic climate was represented by the Rhymers' Club, to which Yeats belonged, and Yeats was a personal and poetical admirer of William Morris. Opposed or related to this and the Tennysonian tradition were such figures as George Meredith, the strenuous outdoor prophet of nature and evolution, whose *Day of the Daughter of Hades* (1883) stands in suggestive contrast with Tennyson's slightly later *Demeter and Persephone* (1887); Robert Bridges, whose mythological dramas and long narrative, *Eros & Psyche,* are for the most part rather pallid and precious; and Sturge Moore, who combined the visual quality of a graphic artist with philosophical seriousness.[18] Outside our mythological domain were such diverse figures as Hardy, Kipling, and Hopkins (the last almost unknown until the 1920's); and some writers were increasingly receptive to influences ranging from Donne to modern French poetry. Thus there were many signs of discontent with effete Romanticism, but a radically fresh start was rather delayed than promoted by the Imagist and Georgian phases. The fresh start came with Yeats, Eliot, and Pound, who also treated classical myth in distinctly modern and masterful ways; and it seems better to look as closely as we can at some bits of their work, however familiar these are, than to catalogue a crowd of good but lesser poets and poems.

For Yeats, who early and deliberately steeped himself in Irish folklore, classical myth was not shopworn literary furniture but a natural, integral part of the true world of the popular and pagan imagination, even though it was to be a

---

[18]The mythological poems of Meredith, Bridges, and Sturge Moore are discussed in D. Bush, *Romantic Tradition*. General books on the latter two are: Albert J. Guérard, *Robert Bridges: A Study of Traditionalism in Poetry* (Cambridge, Mass., 1942) ; F. L. Gwynn, *Sturge Moore and the Life of Art* (Lawrence, Kansas, 1951) .

minor element in his poetry.[19] The early *Song of the Happy Shepherd* (1885) carried on Romantic and Pre-Raphaelite

[19]The briefest discussion of Yeats must be indebted to many books and essays, and, partly for the sake of later reference, it seems best to give here an alphabetical list (which of course does not include all the good criticism), preceded by a few of Yeats's own books. Unless another place is mentioned, all the books were published in New York or London or in both.

Yeats: *Autobiographies* (New York, Macmillan, 1927); *Collected Poems* (New York, Macmillan, 1956: 1965 printing, cited as *C.P.*); *Oxford Book Of Modern Verse*, ed. Yeats (New York, Oxford University Press, 1936); *A Vision* (London, Macmillan, 1962).

R. P. Blackmur, two essays, in *Form & Value in Modern Poetry* (1957); Cleanth Brooks, essays in *Modern Poetry and the Tradition* (1939; repr. in Hall and Steinmann, below) and *The Hidden God* (New Haven, 1963); R. A. Brower, *The Fields of Light* (1951), pp. 83-88; Denis Donoghue and J. R. Mulryne, eds., *An Honoured Guest: New Essays on W. B. Yeats* (1965-1966); Richard Ellmann, *Yeats: The Man and the Masks* (1948, 1958), *The Identity of Yeats* (1954 and, with a new full preface, 1964); Edward Engelberg, *The Vast Design: Patterns in W. B. Yeats's Aesthetic* (Toronto, 1964); Northrop Frye, "Yeats and the Language of Symbolism," *UTQ* 17 (1947-1948), pp. 1-17 (repr. in *Fables of Identity*, 1963), and an essay on the *Vision* in Donoghue and Mulryne, above; James Hall and M. Steinmann, eds., *The Permanence of Yeats: Selected Criticism* (1950); T. R. Henn, *The Lonely Tower: Studies in the Poetry of W. B. Yeats* (1950; rev. and enlarged, 1965); G. Hough, *The Last Romantics* (1949), pp. 216-262; A. Norman Jeffares, *W. B. Yeats: Man and Poet* (1949; 2nd ed., London, 1962, New York, 1966); A. N. Jeffares and K. G. W. Cross, eds., *In Excited Reverie: A Centenary Tribute to William Butler Yeats* (1965); F. Kermode, *Romantic Image* (1959); G. Melchiori, *The Whole Mystery of Art: Pattern into Poetry in the Work of W. B. Yeats* (1960); Thomas W. Parkinson, *W. B. Yeats: Self-Critic* (Berkeley, 1951), *W. B. Yeats: The Later Poetry (ibid., 1964)*; B. Rajan, *W. B. Yeats: A Critical Introduction* (1965); B. L. Reid, *William Butler Yeats: The Lyric of Tragedy* (Norman, Okla., 1958); M. I. Seiden, *William Butler Yeats: The Poet as a Mythmaker* (East Lansing, 1962); Jon Stallworthy, *Between the Lines: Yeats's Poetry in the Making* (Oxford, 1963); Amy G. Stock, *W. B. Yeats: His Poetry and Thought* (Cambridge, 1961); J. Unterecker, *A Reader's Guide to William Butler Yeats* (1959); J. Unterecker, ed., *Yeats: A Collection of Critical Essays* (Englewood Cliffs, N.J., 1963); P. Ure, *Yeats* (1963); Helen H. Vendler, *Yeats's Vision and the Later Plays* (Cambridge, Mass., 1963); A. Wade, *A Bibliography of the Writings of W. B. Yeats* (1958); Thomas R. Whitaker, *Swan and Shadow: Yeats's Dialogue with History* (Chapel Hill, 1964); F. A. C. Wilson, *W. B. Yeats and Tradition* (1958), *Yeats's Iconography* (1960); Yvor Winters, *The Poetry of W. B. Yeats* (Denver, 1960); Alex Zwerdling, *Yeats and the Heroic Ideal* (1965).

We are not concerned with the debated question of Yeats's debt to the French Symbolists, but, because of another connection, we might note his letter to Sir Maurice Bowra (printed in the latter's *Memories 1898-1939* (London, 1966), pp. 240-241) in which he minimized that debt but said he had been greatly influenced by the first half of Arthur Hallam's review of Tennyson's 1830 volume *(Writings of Arthur Hallam*, ed. T. H. V. Motter (New York and London, 1943), pp. 182-198). Here—to enlarge upon Yeats—Hallam had exalted the poetry of "beauty" and "sensation" (Shelley, Keats, Tennyson) above that of reflection (Wordsworth); Hallam was, for the moment, a prophet of art for art's sake. To return to the letter, Yeats defended the Nineties, against common disparagement, as a period of liberating vigor.

tradition in exalting dreams and art ("Words alone are certain good") and in lamenting the encroachments of science:

> The woods of Arcady are dead,
> And over is their antique joy;
> Of old the world on dreaming fed;
> Grey Truth is now her painted toy;
> Yet still she turns her restless head. . . .[20]

We may think again of Blake and Coleridge and Wordsworth and the young Tennyson, whose reaction against scientific rationalism was paralleled, emotionally, by Yeats's reaction to Huxley and Tyndall,[21] which left his religious and symbolist temperament to the resources of his imagination and Celtic myth and some more occult aids; he came to see a fatal split in man's consciousness, beginning in the Renaissance and deepening with seventeenth-century science, whereas Greek and medieval and some Renaissance poets had embodied unity of being.[22] Yeats's few early references to classical myth were in the contemporary convention and mostly associated with the fall of Troy and with the romantic love of women and beauty. But vague Pre-Raphaelite glamor might be freshened by Irish allusion: "Troy passed away in one high funeral gleam, /And Usna's children died" (The Rose of the World, 1892);[23]

---

[20]The Song of the Happy Shepherd (C.P., p. 7). The poem was first printed in 1885 as an epilogue to an Arcadian play, The Island of Statues, and The Seeker. E. Engelberg links it with Pater's "Winckelmann" and "Conclusion" (The Renaissance), recalling Pater's belief that Greek serenity is gone for ever and that the fevered modern world can achieve salvation only through art ("He too was in Arcadia," In Excited Reverie, ed. Jeffares and Cross, n. 19 above: pp. 85-86).

[21]For Huxley et al., see Yeats, Autobiographies (New York, 1927), pp. 74, 97, 142.

[22]On the split in consciousness which left man "passive before a mechanized nature" (Yeats, Oxford Book Of Modern Verse, p. xxvii), see, e.g., Yeats, Autobiographies (New York, 1927), pp. 237, 359 f., A Vision (London, 1962), pp. 255, 290-296; R. Ellmann, Identity of Yeats, p. 24; P. Ure, Yeats, p. 65; Engelberg, Vast Design, pp. 11 f., etc.; Zwerdling, Yeats and the Heroic Ideal, pp. 1-25, etc. (these critics all cited in n. 19 above).

[23]D. Daiches, In Excited Reverie, ed. Jeffares and Cross (n. 19 above), pp. 61-65.

and Helen, the Pre-Raphaelite fatal woman, Yeats saw as a mythological Maud Gonne.[24]

We must take for granted the wide variety of private and public, literary, theatrical, and philosophical experience that nourished Yeats's growth from an Irish Pre-Raphaelite into the greatest poet—as many would join Eliot[25] in saying—of the modern world. His emergence from the Celtic twilight became apparent in his volumes of 1910 and 1914, and most of his finest poetry was written in the 1920's and 1930's, in the last twenty years of his life. The vaguely emotive rhetoric of deliquescent Romanticism gave place by degrees to an individual idiom of rich and resonant force and economy; if Yeats's language, syntax, and rhythms had a colloquial strain, still the total effect was a grand manner that most other modern poets could hardly attempt.

He became conscious with increasing intensity of senses and imaginative powers at their height, of the passion, courage, and pride of the untamed natural man, of the approach of decrepit age and the horror of withering into truth and wisdom, of the conflict between the unbaptized poetry of aristocratic self-assertion "In all the vigour of its blood"[26] and surrender to the austere peace or the bloodless transcendentalism of

---

[24]Yeats's references to Helen of Troy are collected and commented upon by G. Melchiori (n. 19 above), pp. 114-132. In comparison with symbolic implications of the swan, "his treatment of the Helen figure appears much more inconsistent, confused, and at times purely casual" (pp. 114-115), perhaps, Melchiori suggests, because Helen as the fatal woman was such a commonplace in contemporary verse; he cites Mario Praz, *The Romantic Agony* (1933), especially chapters IV and V. But Melchiori finds Yeats's Helen becoming "the essence of poetic vision, and at the same time . . . a reminder of the decay of the flesh," "beauty and . . . frenzy," "destruction and conflict, but also the union of opposites, the union of all beliefs. . ." (p. 130). *Cf.* H. H. Vendler (n. 19 above), pp. 36-39.

Donald Davie *(An Honoured Guest,* ed. Donoghue and Mulryne, n. 19 above: pp. 83-84) remarks on the homely—and Jonsonian—treatment of myth in the allusion to Aphrodite and her "bandy-leggèd smith" in *A Prayer for My Daughter* (1919).

[25]T. S. Eliot, "The Poetry of Yeats," *Southern Review* 7 (1941-1942): pp. 442-454; repr. in Hall and Steinmann, *The Permanence of Yeats* (n. 19 above), pp. 331-343, and, with some changes, in Eliot's *On Poetry and Poets* (1957).

[26]Yeats, *Tom the Lunatic (C.P.,* pp. 263-264).

Platonic and Plotinian philosophy—all the tormenting disunity in man's own nature ("The fury and the mire of human veins"[27]) and in the strange world he inhabits. Yeats's many "masks," however variable, were all genuine, and no less genuine were his efforts to understand and unify the discords. In *Sailing to Byzantium* (1926)—a poem that invites contrast with Tennyson's *Ulysses*—Yeats turns away from the temporal flux of all animal and human existence to the artifice of eternity, the ideal unified culture symbolized by Byzantium; yet Byzantine art is to tell, with all-embracing knowledge, of the changing world, and—as with Keats's *Grecian Urn*—it remains an ironic question whether the poet can or really would transcend his human instincts and limitations.

Yeats's recognition of conflict and turbulence within and outside himself, and his forging of a new strong rhetoric commensurate with that, led, not to the casting off of either Celtic or classical myth, but to a new and original power in the use of it. The Homer who had been a sort of William Morris became a larger poet of the human condition:

> What theme had Homer but original sin?
> . . . .
> Homer is my example and his unchristened heart.[28]

The Irish troubles helped to bring Troy out of romantic tapestry into living experience; and the city and its fall took a place in the cyclical theory of history that Yeats set forth in *A Vision* (1925; second, revised edition, 1937), that intricate, occult "system" which, if not a substantial philosophical or religious creed, provided a coherent pattern of symbolic images. Their meaning and coherence depend far more upon the poet's individual feeling and imagination than the mythological symbols of the Renaissance, which were malleable parts of an accepted, strongly ethical body of fable more or less allied with Christian tradition. Although Yvor Winters had some warrant

---

[27] *Byzantium (C.P.,* p. 243).
[28] *Vacillation* viii *(C.P.,* p. 247). See the commentary in Ellmann, *Identity,* pp. 268-274, etc.

for his blunt condemnation of Yeats's "foolish" ideas, there is more illumination of the poetry in Giorgio Melchiori's remark that the poet "projected his personal microcosmos into a macrocosmos, or, in other words, unconsciously made a universe out of his own personality."[29] Symbolic images based on Yeats's arbitrary and erratic pattern of history generally work in his poetry, and even bizarre ones may enhance our central sense of life and mystery; yet the few poems we can look at suggest that the total impact is strongest when the system is least obtrusive.

In Yeats's cyclical (and not always consistent) view of history, the birth and death of Christ brought an era of turbulence, and in *The Second Coming*,[30] a poem evoked by the state of Ireland and the world in 1919, the Christian era is followed by a worse one. The new age of nightmare violence is represented by a sinister beast that "Slouches towards Bethlehem to be born." If for a moment we put aside Yeats's theory, we might say that the climactic shock of this image could have been given by a Christian poet contemplating, like Yeats, the timeless theme of bloody anarchy unloosed upon the world. Two lines of plain statement, we may note, echo that "sacred book" of Yeats's earlier days, Shelley's *Prometheus Unbound:*

> The best lack all conviction, while the worst
> Are full of passionate intensity.

The Second Coming brings us to our more direct concern, *Two Songs from a Play*,[31] published by themselves in *The*

[29]Yvor Winters (n. 19 above), pp. 4, 7, 8, 9; Melchiori (n. 19 above), p. 112.

[30]*The Second Coming* (*C.P.*, p. 184). The lines from *Prometheus Unbound* are quoted above in II; the very audible echo has often been noted. Yeats's phrase "sacred book" is in *Autobiographies* (n. 19 above), p. 108. One full analysis is D. Weeks's "Image and Idea in Yeats's *The Second Coming*," *PMLA* 63 (1948): pp. 281-292. See also Ellmann, *Identity*, pp. 257-260, Stallworthy (n. 19 above), pp. 16-25; etc.; and the comments of C. C. O'Brien in his full study of Yeats in politics (*In Excited Reverie*, pp. 274-278: n. 19 above).

[31]The *Two Songs* (*C.P.*, pp. 210-211) are discussed by R. A. Brower (n. 19 above) and more or less in the standard books on Yeats, e.g., Ellmann, *Identity*, pp. 260-263, Unterecker, *Reader's Guide* (n. 19 above), pp. 185-187. The process of composition and revision of the play is shown by C. B. Bradford, *Yeats at Work* (Carbondale, 1965), pp. 237-267.

Tower (1928), but forming parts of *The Resurrection*, in which a Dionysian festival is a background for the risen Christ. The god of wine, the inaugurator of orgiastic rites, was an age-old symbol of man's instinctual urges, and the idea had been notably philosophized in Nietzsche's *Birth of Tragedy*, in the antinomy between the daemonic impulses of Dionysus and the rational control of Apollo.[32] Yeats's antinomy dissolves into a similarity or parallel between Dionysus and Christ.[33] The first *Song* begins with the god's death, which was annually celebrated along with his rebirth:

> I saw a staring virgin stand
> Where holy Dionysus died,
> And tear the heart out of his side,
> And lay the heart upon her hand
> And bear that beating heart away;
> And then did all the Muses sing
> Of Magnus Annus at the spring,
> As though God's death were but a play.

The stanza implies the primitive harmonious unity of Greek religion, drama, and poetry, of Greek culture in general. The "staring virgin" is, primarily, the goddess Athene, who carried the heart of the dead Dionysus to Zeus.[34] There is a veiled suggestion of Easter and of the eucharistic body and blood of Christ.

---

[32]"In Nietzsche's mature years the real opposition is not Dionysus versus Apollo, but the Apolline Dionysus versus Christ" (Erich Heller, *The Disinherited Mind* (Cambridge, Bowes & Bowes, 1952), p. 110). One anticipation of Nietzsche's early antinomy is Coleridge's remark that Bacchus is not merely the jolly god of wine but "the symbol of that power which acts without our consciousness from the vital energies of nature, as Apollo was the symbol of our intellectual consciousness" (*Coleridge's Shakespearean Criticism*, ed. T. M. Raysor (Cambridge, Mass., 1930) 2, p. 263; *cf.* 1: pp. 184-185, 2: p. 7). See also Henry Hatfield, *Aesthetic Paganism* (below, Bibliography, II), p. 12; G. C. Monsman, *Pater's Portraits* (n. 2 above), pp. 16 f., etc.; and, for the ancient beginnings, E. R. Dodds, *The Greeks and the Irrational* (Berkeley, 1951); John Pollard, "Dionysus," *Seers, Shrines and Sirens* (London, 1965), pp. 78-92.

[33]M. L. Rosenthal remarks: "Christ resurrected is but the fusion of pure physicality and pure spirituality mysteriously embodied. It is not the New Testament Jesus, but Dionysus reborn who ushers in a new phase of history" (*The Modern Poets* (New York, Oxford University Press, 1960), p. 46). *Cf.* Ellmann, *Identity*, p. 260; Whitaker (n. 19 above), pp. 104-107. Mrs. Vendler (n. 19 above: pp. 178 f.) sees the two deaths and resurrections as "parallel, not similar."

[34] Footnote on page 73.

The second stanza, taking a wider sweep, brings us to Rome
and the beginning of the Christian era:

> Another Troy must rise and set,
> Another lineage feed the crow,
> Another Argo's painted prow
> Drive to a flashier bauble yet.
> The Roman empire stood appalled:
> It dropped the reins of peace and war
> When that fierce virgin and her Star
> Out of the fabulous darkness called.[35]

---

[34]Brower (n. 19 above) and Ellmann (*Identity*, p. 260) name Athene, the
latter citing Frazer's *Golden Bough* (abridged one-volume edition (New York,
Macmillan, 1922), pp. 388-389; 1st ed. (1890), 1: p. 323). F. A. C. Wilson
(*W. B. Yeats and Tradition*, London: V. Gollancz, 1958, pp. 60-62) cites Thomas
Taylor's *Dissertation* for the saving of the god's heart as "a symbol of his
eventual liberation and resurrection into the spiritual world." Yeats may have
met the image in the similar tale of Here (who of course was not a virgin)
mentioned at the end of Pater's essay on Dionysus (*Greek Studies* (London,
Macmillan, 1928), p. 41), which included Yeats's "beating": "Meanwhile Here,
full of her vengeance, brings to Zeus the heart of the child, which she had
snatched, still beating, from the hands of the Titans." Whitaker (n. 19 above:
pp. 104 and 313, n. 34) refers to Here and Pater but does not quote him; he
cites Demeter also in Frazer, 389. Cf. Yeats, *Vision* (1962), p. 272. For the
eating of flesh see Pater, "Dionysus" (*Greek Studies*, pp. 37, 40-41), Frazer, pp.
388-389, and, for modern scholarly inquiries, Ivan M. Linforth, *The Arts of
Orpheus* (Berkeley, 1941), chap. 5, "Myth of the Dismemberment of Dionysus,"
pp. 307-364, and J. Pollard (n. 32 above), who barely touches this item.

On the last line of the first stanza see Whitaker, p. 107. But for the context
the line might suggest that Yeats was for the moment writing in the spirit of
Matthew Arnold's comments on the inadequacy of the Greek religion of the
senses as represented by the festival of Adonis in Theocritus, *Id.* 15 ("Pagan
and Mediaeval Religious Sentiment," *Essays in Criticism*, First Series).

[35]In line 14 of the first *Song* (C.P., 210) "reins" is misprinted as "reigns."

Did Yeats remember Arnold's picture (*Obermann Once More*, 125 f.) of
Rome's reaction to the birth of Christianity?

> 'She veiled her eagles, snapped her sword,
> And laid her sceptre down;
> Her stately purple she abhorred,
> And her imperial crown.

> 'She broke her flutes, she stopped her sports,
> Her artists could not please;
> She tore her books, she shut her courts,
> She fled her palaces;

> 'Lust of the eye and pride of life
> She left it all behind,
> And hurried, torn with inward strife,
> The wilderness to find. . . .'

These lines link themselves with a long poetic tradition. In Virgil's Messianic eclogue the vision of a new golden age and the return of the virgin Astraea (goddess of justice) is shadowed by the thought of recurring sin and war: "A second Tiphys shall then arise, and a second Argo to carry chosen heroes; a second warfare, too, shall there be, and again shall a great Achilles be sent to Troy."[36] Along with that Yeats remembered the last chorus of Shelley's *Hellas,* itself a partial imitation of Virgil:

> The world's great age begins anew,
>   The golden years return. . . .
>
> A loftier Argo cleaves the main,
>   Fraught with a later prize;
> Another Orpheus sings again,
>   And loves, and weeps, and dies.
> A new Ulysses leaves once more
> Calypso for his native shore.

But Shelley cannot sustain his bright vision of another Athens and the reign of freedom and love; he ends with a despairing prophecy of continued hate and war and death. Yeats's echoes of his forerunners only accentuate his skeptical and even savage ironies. "Another Argo's painted prow" and "flashier bauble yet" have far more ferocity than the "painted toy" of the *Song of the Happy Shepherd.*

The pagan parallel with Christian tradition is carried on in the ambiguous last lines. Peace in the Roman empire at the time of Christ's birth had been celebrated in Milton's *Nativity,* and "that fierce virgin and her Star" links the Virgin Mary and the star of Bethlehem with the "staring virgin" of the first line. But Rome had been darkened by its own imperial expansion and by its assimilation of eastern religious cults, and Christ brought a religion of compassion, self-renunciation, and hope, which nevertheless ushered in an era of violence:

---

[36]Virgil, *Ecl.* iv. 34-36 (Loeb Classical Library). See Yeats, *Vision* (1962), pp. 243-244. Ellmann *(Identity,* p. 261) collects Yeats's references to the Virgilian prophecy, made over thirty years, 1896-1925.

> In pity for man's darkening thought
> He walked that room and issued thence
> In Galilean turbulence;
> The Babylonian starlight brought
> A fabulous, formless darkness in;
> Odour of blood when Christ was slain
> Made all Platonic tolerance vain
> And vain all Doric discipline.

In Yeats's historical scheme the civilization represented by Babylonian mathematics and astrology was followed by the twenty centuries of Greece and Rome (2000 B.C. to A.D. 1),[37] which attained the rational thought and moral discipline of Plato and Sparta. This era in turn was destroyed by the birth of Christ and Christianity, described by the philosopher Proclus as "fabulous, formless darkness."[38] "Odour of blood when Christ was slain" implies the anti-intellectual subversion of Greek order and unity of being.

The imaginative, verbal, and rhythmical force and splendor of these stanzas do take possession of us, yet rather, it seems to me, as a tissue of images than as a coherent expression of a viable theme. If they are far stronger and more complex than Swinburne's neopagan attack on the "pale Galilean," their ideas are perhaps not much more satisfying. But the last stanza of the second *Song*, added in 1931, leaves "history" to declare in half-generalized terms the transitoriness of all human endeavor. The ending, though, is less negation than affirmation:

> Whatever flames upon the night
> Man's own resinous heart has fed.

Here, in images that recall the earlier "darkness" and the pine torches of Dionysian rites, Yeats sees the tragic essence

---

[37]For the twenty centuries see *A Vision* (1962), pp. 267 f.

[38]For the philosopher Proclus see *A Vision*, p. 278; Ellmann, *Identity*, p. 262. By way of contrast, it might be noted that, for reasons too complex for summary here, J. D. Rea *(MP* 26 (1928-1929): p. 211) took Proclus to be the particular figure behind Wordsworth's "Pagan suckled in a creed outworn," in the sonnet quoted above in II.

of life in the brief creative fire of human passion.[39] The line in the early *Happy Shepherd*—"Of old the world on dreaming fed"—has gained a new depth.

A partly similar theme inspired one of the most powerful sonnets in the language, *Leda and the Swan* (1923-1925), but this poem, though related to Yeats's eccentric system, can be pretty fully grasped independently of that; while its endless suggestiveness has invited endless elucidation, it does not, like the *Two Songs,* require a panoply of footnotes. The sonnet is, by the way, a prime example of drastic revision or re-creation.[40]

> A sudden blow: the great wings beating still
> Above the staggering girl, her thighs caressed
> By the dark webs, her nape caught in his bill,
> He holds her helpless breast upon his breast.
>
> How can those terrified vague fingers push
> The feathered glory from her loosening thighs?
> And how can body, laid in that white rush,
> But feel the strange heart beating where it lies?
>
> A shudder in the loins engenders there
> The broken wall, the burning roof and tower
> And Agamemnon dead.
>   Being so caught up,
> So mastered by the brute blood of the air,
> Did she put on his knowledge with his power
> Before the indifferent beak could let her drop?

The sonnet is potent enough simply as the re-creation of a mythic event; but, from the explosive opening through the tactual immediacy of the description, the tissue of sensations— as felt by Leda, not the swan—initiates a train of epic and tragic consequences. Fifteen years earlier, writing in *No Sec-*

---

[39]Brower, *Fields of Light,* pp. 87-88; Whitaker (n. 19 above), pp. 106-107, 313, n. 38. The last stanza was added in 1931 (Ellmann, *Identity,* p. 260). See B. L. Reid (n. 19 above), pp. 187-189; H. H. Vendler (n. 19 above), pp. 184-185. Commenting on the last stanza, Mrs. Vendler sees the theme of Yeats's play as "the waning of one source of imaginative strength and the revivifying appearance of a new creative force. . . . The stanza is affirming the transiency of any imaginative form." She similarly interprets *The Second Coming* (pp. 98-102) and *Leda and the Swan* (n. 42 below) as concerned with the artist's imaginative experience.

[40]For the successive versions of *Leda* see Ellmann, *Identity,* pp. 176-179.

ond Troy of the beautiful and single-minded revolutionist, Maud Gonne, Yeats had ended with a reverberating question: "Was there another Troy for her to burn?" But the sonnet is far larger in scope, wholly dramatic and impersonal, and carries an accumulated wealth of meaning. It was first conceived, Yeats said, when he was asked for a poem by an Irish political review. He had thought of modern culture as exhausted and felt that "Nothing is now possible but some movement, or birth from above, preceded by some violent annunciation";[41] however, thoughts of Leda had driven out politics and fastened on "the annunciation that founded Greece."

The Christian Michelangelo, in a painting which has been taken as one of Yeats's many "sources,"[42] expressed, without

---

[41]Yeats, *The Cat and the Moon and Certain Poems* (Dublin, Cuala Press, 1924), p. 37. The passage is quoted in full by, e.g., Jeffares, *W. B. Yeats* (n. 19 above), pp. 223-224; P. Allt and R. K. Alspach, *Variorum Edition of the Poems of W. B. Yeats* (New York, 1957), p. 828; H. H. Vendler (n. 19 above), p. 108. *Cf.* Yeats, *Vision*, "Book V: Dove or Swan," pp. 267-268, etc.

[42]G. Melchiori elaborately examined possible literary and pictorial sources and the significance of Yeats's symbolism ("Leda and the Swan: The Genesis of Yeats' Poem," *English Miscellany* 7 (1956): pp. 147-239; enlarged in *The Whole Mystery of Art* (London, 1960), pp. 73-199). He took Michelangelo's painting of Leda as "the main inspiration" (p. 159; *cf.* p. 139). Charles Madge *(Times Literary Supplement,* July 20, 1962) proposed, as much closer than Michelangelo to Yeats's poem, an ancient bas-relief in the British Museum: "Every detail of the [first] six lines . . . seems to be taken directly from the sculpture." Melchiori and H. R. Williamson agreed with this judgment *(ibid.,* August 3 and 31). Charles Gullans *(ibid.,* Nov. 9, 1962) found a pictorial source "in detail just as close to the sonnet" in a woodcut bookplate designed by Sturge Moore; however, he questioned Yeats's need of "any pictorial referent" and renewed the idea of his literary debt to Moore's ode *To Leda (To Leda and Other Odes,* 1904) in the prophetic relating of Leda's experience to the fall of Troy and other data. Madge *(ibid.,* Nov. 16) was not convinced and held by his bas-relief. R. Ellmann *(Identity* (1964 ed.), preface; *cf.* pp. 176-179) deprecated the notion of visual models and stressed the expression in the sonnet of characteristically Yeatsian ideas. T. R. Henn, who endorses Madge, gives a succinct summary of the sonnet's symbols and meanings *(The Lonely Tower* (1965 ed.), pp. xviii, 255-257).

Mrs. Vendler (p. 107: n. 19 above) stresses the idea that the central concern of the sonnet is "whether a special knowledge attaches to the conferred power of artistic creation." Along with discussions in the other standard books on Yeats, some studies of *Leda* are: pp. 617-620 in A. Stein, *Sewanee Review* 57 (1949): pp. 603-626; Jane D. Reid, *Journal of Aesthetics and Art Criticism* 11 (1952-1953): pp. 378-389, and L. R. Rind, *Chicago Review* 7 (1953): pp. 13-17, both on Yeats and Rilke; H. Trowbridge, *MP* 51 (1953-1954): pp. 118-129; L. Spitzer, *ibid.,* pp. 271-276 (repr. in his *Essays on English and American Literature,* ed. A. Hatcher (Princeton, 1962)).

irony, "the suave perfection of the union of human and divine";[43] the Christian Spenser, whose several swans are prime sources, put a voluptuous picture of Leda and the swan among tapestries representing romantic, sensual love.[44] For the non-Christian Yeats the momentary encounter between the amorous, omnipotent, omniscient Zeus and a helpless girl is by intention and implication a pagan parallel or antithesis to Mary's conception of Christ. It engenders the long span of history that begins with the birth of the sisters Helen and Clytemnestra, Paris' abduction of Helen, the war and the fall of Troy, the return of Agamemnon and his murder at the hands of Clytemnestra. The re-creation of the myth and the sequence of tragic events involve more general ideas, most immediately "the destructiveness of sexual passion, . . . its power to upheave the world."[45] But this moment of violence is also a miracle, a union of god and mortal, and the last lines suggest philosophic questions which take many forms in Yeats: the antinomies, especially in artistic creation, between knowledge and power, mind and body, eternal and temporal; the relation of man's imperfect physical and spiritual being to both the brute indifferent vitality of nature and whatever of "spirit" is in or above nature; the presence in man, as in the universe, of opposites, of creative and destructive forces and the possibility or impossibility of either fusing or transcending them. As a recent critic says, "No less than the orthodox Christian, Yeats needed the symbol of incarnation to focus the paradoxes of a world in which every act is also a suffering, every creation a discovery, every death a rebirth."[46] We may wonder whether, in the question "Did she put on his knowledge with his power . . . ?," the "pagan" poet is ironically echoing St. Paul's exhorta-

---

[43]Ellmann, *Identity* (1964), p. vi.

[44]Spenser, *The Faerie Queene* III. xi. 32. Yeats may have got hints from Spenser's "rusht," the prominence given to the bird's breast, and the military metaphor in "invade" (Melchiori, p. 113). Melchiori also (pp. 86, 107-108) quotes the *Prothalamion* (39-45) and *Ruines of Time* (589-602) and notes Yeats's apparent echoes in other poems; he concludes (p. 109) that "the image of the swan was mainly of Spenserian origin." See n. 42 above.

[45]Ellmann, *Identity* (1964), p. viii. *Cf.* Vivienne Koch's study of the last poems, *W. B. Yeats: The Tragic Phase* (London, 1951).

[46]Whitaker (n. 19 above), p. 107.

tions to "put on the new man"—as Milton, with another kind of irony, had Satan urge Eve and Adam "by putting off / Human, to put on gods"; at any rate the phrase calls up a very different creed.[47]

Since we began with Yeats's conventional romantic allusions to Troy, we might complete our small "gyre" with one brief declaration of acceptance of life and history, a tragic vision partly akin to that of Keats's two *Hyperions*—though Keats could not have shared Yeats's sometimes Nietzschean gaiety:

> Hector is dead and there's a light in Troy;
> We that look on but laugh in tragic joy.[48]

We may be further reminded that a good part of Yeats's later poetry enforces what the young Keats had tried to say even in *Endymion,* that the way to the ideal lies through the real, transcendental moments being rare. The giant Antaeus, who for Spenser and Milton represented sin and Satan, symbolized for Yeats the poet's life-giving contact with the soil, the vitality of the noble and the beggar-man.[49]

T. S. Eliot, like the older Yeats, grew up in the post-Romantic tradition and, like Yeats, achieved artistic and spiritual maturity partly through very eclectic assimilation of literature and thought ancient and modern, Eastern and Western. Instead, however, of Yeats's long Pre-Raphaelite apprenticeship and occult interests, Eliot had an orthodox literary and philosophical education which might have shaped a mere traditionalist. But his early poems, some written before his graduation from Harvard in 1910, show him as already a modernist in

---

[47]For putting off the old man and putting on the new, see Eph. iv. 22-24, Col. iii. 9-10, 1 Cor. xv. 53; Milton, *Paradise Lost* ix. 713-714. Spitzer *(Essays,* p. 11: n. 42 above) quotes the repeated "put on incorruption" and "put on immortality" from 1 Cor. v. 51-54.

[48]Yeats, The Gyres *(C.P.,* p. 291); Ellmann, *Identity,* pp. 91-98; B. L. Reid (n. 19 above), pp. 88-91, 211-213, 255; Whitaker (n. 19 above), pp. 275-281; Henn, *Lonely Tower* (1965), pp. 319, 322; J. H. Miller, "W. B. Yeats," *Poets of Reality* (Cambridge, Mass., 1965), pp. 119-124; and R. Ellmann *(Eminent Domain* (New York, 1967), p. 19), who sees in Yeats's lines the influence of Wilde.

[49]For Antaeus in Spenser and Milton see above, I, n. 35. Yeats's allusion is in *The Municipal Gallery Revisited (C.P.,* p. 318).

technique and sensibility:[50] a Jamesian American of Puritan heritage who experienced the Europe of the years before, during, and after the First World War, a poet who attained revolutionary originality through rigorous self-discipline, through study of a diverse combination of English and Continental writers old and new. And from the first he recorded, with both wit and compassion, the drab, meaningless monotony of everyday life, genteel and plebeian. Moreover, the kind of order the Irish Yeats arrived at might be said to start from a sanctification of man's natural instincts, an un-Christian or anti-Christian, half-barbaric joy in the passion, pride, and human self-sufficiency of aristocrat, peasant, and poet; whereas the expatriate American declared himself in mid-career a classicist, royalist, and Anglo-Catholic, and the religious seed or gleam manifest in his early poems became the symbolic rose and fire of *Four Quartets*—both favorite symbols of Yeats but not carrying the same meaning. There is a great gulf between Eliot's *The Rock* and Yeats's "Old Rocky Face" *(The Gyres)*, however the latter is interpreted. Yeats's ancient poet-hero was the "unchristened" Homer; Eliot's was Virgil, seen—in a sophisticated way—as the almost Christian poet revered in the Middle Ages.[51]

---

[50]The poems printed in the *Harvard Advocate* of 1907-1910—reprinted in the Eliot number of the *Advocate* (December, 1938) and in *Poems Written in Early Youth* (London, 1967) —suggest his transition from late Victorian romanticism to modernism (one poem of 1910 is "After J. Laforgue"). Of one 14-line piece the *TLS* (June 1, 1967) remarked: "There is sexual symbolism and disgust in the Swinburnean 'Circe's Palace.' " The comment seems to me to read both the later Eliot and Swinburne into an innocent, half-ninetyish, half-modern poem.

[51]Along with the evidence in Eliot's prose and poetry and with general comments in the critics, there are such specific discussions of his classicism as these: A. J. Creedy, "Eliot and the Classics," *Orpheus: Rivista di Umanità* 1 (1954) : pp. 42-58; Robert Fitzgerald, "Generations of Leaves: The poet in the classical tradition," *Perspectives USA*, No. 8 (1954) : pp. 68-85; W. F. J. Knight, "T. S. Eliot as a Classical Scholar," *T. S. Eliot: A Symposium for his Seventieth Birthday*, ed. Neville Braybrooke (London and New York, 1958) : pp. 119-128; D. J. DeLaura, "The Place of the Classics in T. S. Eliot's Christian Humanism," *Hereditas*, ed. F. Will (Austin, 1964) , pp. 155-197; R. W. Janoff, "Eliot and Horace—Aspects of the Intrinsic Classicist," *Cithara* 5, 1 (1965) : pp. 31-44. There are of course numerous discussions of Eliot's use of Greek sources in some of his plays.

In the short satire, *Mr. Apollinax* (1915), the anaemic culture of refined, complacent Bostonians is ruffled—though not for long—by a foreign visitor whose primitive vitality suggests Priapus, a centaur,[52] the goat-god Pan, and Proteus and the symbolic power of the sea. A similar atmosphere and similar and other motifs had been subtly elaborated in *The Love Song of J. Alfred Prufrock* (written in 1910-1911 and published in 1915), which is often taken as the inauguration of modern poetry. The *persona* is at the opposite pole from Yeats's bold upstanding heroes. He reveals himself as a man of elegant cultivation, ironic wit, and morbid self-consciousness who shrinks timidly from life and love and can only, from a distance, covet the capacity for action:

> I should have been a pair of ragged claws
> Scuttling across the floors of silent seas.

Whereas Yeats was to assail decrepitude with lust and rage, the prematurely old Prufrock accepts his unheroic destiny

---

52For the symbolic significance of the centaur, half-man and half-horse, a few references are: Maurice de Guérin's *Le Centaure,* from which Arnold translated extracts in his essay; Sturge Moore, *The Centaur's Booty* (1903); Yeats, *On a Picture of a Black Centaur by Edmund Dulac (The Tower* (1928); *C.P.,* p. 212). Donald Davidson ("Yeats and the Centaur," *Southern Review* 7 (1941-1942): pp. 510-516; repr. in Hall and Steinmann, *The Permanence of Yeats* (1950): pp. 278-285) took as his text Yeats's saying: "I thought that all art should be a Centaur finding in the popular lore its back and strong legs" *(Autobiographies,* New York, Macmillan (1927): p. 236).

One may wonder whether Eliot's "I heard the beat of centaur's hoofs over the hard turf" echoes Meredith's "Hears the heart of wildness beat/Like a centaur's hoof on sward" *(The Woods of Westermain, Poetical Works of George Meredith,* ed. G. M. Trevelyan (London, 1912), p. 196). *Mr. Apollinax* is discussed, e.g., by Elizabeth Drew, *T. S. Eliot: The Design of his Poetry* (New York, 1949), pp. 25-30, and Grover Smith, *T. S. Eliot's Poetry and Plays* (Chicago, 1956), pp. 32-33.

Genesius Jones *(Approach to the Purpose: A Study of the Poetry of T. S. Eliot* (London, Hodder and Stoughton, 1964)) can be enlightening and sometimes puzzling: e.g., he turns Eliot's hyacinths into "the god Hyacinth of the Vegetation Cults," who, "as *The Golden Bough* makes clear, is a figure of transcendent Eros, Agape and Charis" (pp. 92, 237, 289, etc.). I do not see warrant for this either in Eliot or in Frazer's chapter on Hyacinth *(The Golden Bough* (New York, 1935), 5). As if Eliot had been from the first a committed Christian, Father Jones applies from the first that triple conception of Eros, Agape, and Charis, which in *Mr. Apollinax* "are presented in debased form"; the hero, though "lionised by the vapid intelligentsia, . . . is presented as a pathetic ignoramus," a creature of "sterile laughter" (pp. 95-96, 203). Surely that is not what Eliot meant at all; that is not it, at all.

with melancholy candor and futile longing, though not without touches of trivial self-assertion. A poem that began with
a picture of fog (in St. Louis) ends with another kind of
picture:

> I shall wear white flannel trousers, and walk upon the beach.
> I have heard the mermaids singing, each to each.
>
> I do not think that they will sing to me.
>
> I have seen them riding seaward on the waves
> Combing the white hair of the waves blown back
> When the wind blows the water white and black.
>
> We have lingered in the chambers of the sea
> By sea-girls wreathed with seaweed red and brown
> Till human voices wake us, and we drown.

In this conclusion the poem for the first time becomes
"poetical," in a romantic dream of the unattainable. The
Homeric sirens (whom the Elizabethans equated with mermaids)[53] traditionally sought to lure heroes from their
high purposes, as in *The Faerie Queene* (II.xii.30-34) and
Samuel Daniel's lyric, *Ulysses and the Siren*. Here the tradition
is reversed: the anti-hero does not think that the sirens will
sing to him, but his imagination escapes into a momentary
illusion of natural freedom and fulfillment—an idea nearer to
Arnold's *New Sirens* than to Homer.[54] For a contrast with

---

[53] W. P. Mustard, "Siren-Mermaid," *MLN* 23 (1908) : pp. 21-24; Lotspeich
(above, I, n. 17), "Mermaids"; Starnes and Talbert (below, Bibliography, I),
pp. 42, 108-110. See above, II, n. 40, for the references given by H. Rahner and
W. B. Stanford.

[54] The last lines of *Prufrock* Leonard Unger explains thus: "We bungle our
adventures in the actual world because we are out of our true element, having
strayed from the sea-girls and sea-chambers, the dreamworld that is an
approach to spiritual reality" *(Southern Review* 7 (1941-1942) : p. 671; *T. S.
Eliot: A Selected Critique*, ed. L. Unger (New York, Rinehart, 1948), p. 377).

Edmund Wilson *(Axel's Castle* (New York, 1931), pp. 97-98) and many later
critics have discussed Laforgue's influence on *Prufrock* and other poems, e.g.,
E. J. H. Greene, *RLC* 22 (1948) : pp. 363-397 and *T. S. Eliot et la France*
(Paris, 1951), and Warren Ramsey, *Jules Laforgue and the Ironic Inheritance*
(New York, 1953). G. Smith (pp. 301-302, n. 13: see n. 52 above) collects
possible echoes, in the conclusion of *Prufrock*, of Masefield *(Cardigan Bay*, lines
9-12, *Collected Poems* (1923), p. 29), Shakespeare, Chaucer, and Tennyson. S.
Musgrove cites Tennyson's *The Sea-Fairies* (praised by Eliot in his essay on
Tennyson) and especially *The Merman* and *The Mermaid (T. S. Eliot and
Walt Whitman* (Wellington, 1952), p. 43; p. 81 in *T. S. Eliot*, ed. H. Kenner,

Continued on page 83

Eliot we might remember, in Yeats's much later *News for the Delphic Oracle*, the descent from attenuated heavenly love to what—if the watery context allowed—might be called earthy satisfaction:

> Foul goat-head, brutal arm appear,
> Belly, shoulder, bum,
> Flash fishlike; nymphs and satyrs
> Copulate in the foam.[55]

The short poems in quatrains that belong to Eliot's "Gautier period" (1917-1919) work variations on the contrast between heroic or ideal past and sordid present, between wholeness of being and disintegration, health and disease.[56] Such contrasts, however different the focus and technique, recall many poems of Arnold. Tawdry tourists and lovers in modern Venice are seen, in their commercialized cheapness, against the sumptuous and heroic background of Shakespeare's *Antony and Cleopatra* and Antony's ancestral Hercules.[57] A repulsive picture of masculine callousness in a dubious lodginghouse or brothel is introduced with an allusion to Theseus' desertion of Ariadne,

---

Englewood Cliffs, N. J., 1962). Two items perhaps not yet recorded are: Keats's carved angels "With hair blown back" *(Eve of St. Agnes,* line 36); Tennyson's "When the wind blows the foam" *(Œnone,* line 61). Various critics have quoted Gérard de Nerval's "J'ai rêvé dans la grotte ou nage la sirène" *(El Desdichado, Œuvres,* ed. H. Lemaitre (Paris, 1958) I, p. 693), from a sonnet quoted by Eliot in *The Waste Land,* line 429.

[55]Yeats, *News for the Delphic Oracle (C.P.,* p. 324). T. R. Henn *(The Lonely Tower* (ed. 1965), pp. 248-249; *cf.* ed. 1949, pp. 235-236) finds "such startling correspondence that there can be no doubt as to the source," i.e., Poussin's *The Marriage of Peleus and Thetis* (recently retitled as *Acis and Galatea*) in the National Gallery of Ireland. *Cf.* Ellmann, *Identity,* pp. 284-285; D. R. Clark, "Poussin and Yeats's 'News for the Delphic Oracle,'" *Wascana Review* 2 (1967): pp. 33-44.

[56]Edmund Wilson *(Axel's Castle* (1931), p. 100) stressed the presence of this theme in Flaubert, "a great hero of Eliot's, as of . . . Pound's" [see the allusion in *Hugh Selwyn Mauberley*]; but in his attitude toward the contrast, more moral and religious than aesthetic and secular, Eliot may seem akin to Arnold. *Cf.* n. 60 below.

[57]*Burbank with a Baedeker: Bleistein with a Cigar.* For the many writings echoed in the epigraph and text see Grover Smith (n. 52 above), pp. 51-54. R. F. Goheen dealt minutely with echoes of Ovid, Horace, and Virgil in the third stanza *(Sewanee Review* 61 (1953): pp. 109-119). The source of Eliot's allusion to Antony and Hercules is the phrase from *Antony and Cleopatra* (IV. iii. 15-16) quoted above in I.

in high Latinate style.[58] But of course the supreme thing is
the conclusion of *Sweeney Among the Nightingales* (the only
bit of the early Eliot that Yeats, in 1936, could see as "in the
great manner").[59] Several persons in a low dive are plotting to
murder Sweeney, the type, in Eliot's private mythology, of the
sensual human animal; here all the characters are described in
animal terms. In contrast to this vicious scene are, first, the
epigraph, the cry of Aeschylus' Agamemnon as he is stabbed
by his wife, and, second, the grandly ominous images of cosmic
nature, death, and myth. As concrete particulars heighten
vaguely mysterious fear,

> The host with someone indistinct
> Converses at the door apart,
> The nightingales are singing near
> The Convent of the Sacred Heart,
>
> And sang within the bloody wood
> When Agamemnon cried aloud,
> And let their liquid siftings fall
> To stain the stiff dishonoured shroud.

The nightingales and the Convent call up, with marvelous
economy, the two great traditions of Western man, the Greek
and the Christian; and the ironic allusions distinguish—and
perhaps equate—a glamorous crime of the pagan past and a

---

[58]The epigraph to *Sweeney Erect,* from Beaumont and Fletcher, *The Maid's
Tragedy* II. ii. 74-77, points to the allusion to Theseus and Ariadne in the
preceding passage, II. ii. 17-57. See G. Smith, p. 47, and Arthur Mizener's
comment on the poem *(Sewanee Review* 65 (1957) : pp. 41-42; repr. in *T. S.
Eliot,* ed. Hugh Kenner (1962) , pp. 20-21) .

D. E. S. Maxwell *(The Poetry of T. S. Eliot* (London, Routledge & Kegan
Paul, 1952) , p. 81) says that Ariadne is "the goddess of vegetation,
personification of Spring and returning life, symbol of fertility." He
does not give any authority for this interpretation. Maxwell also has "the
perjured sails" refer to Tristan and Isolde: but why not Theseus' sails? *Cf.
periuri . . . viri* in Ovid, *Heroides* x. 76; the other details in Eliot's lines 1-11
might all have been suggested by Ovid's epistle.

[59]W. B. Yeats, *The Oxford Book Of Modern Verse* (New York, Oxford
University Press, 1936) , p. xxii.

squalid crime of the Christian present. [60] We remember the bridging of time and space in Keats's and Arnold's poems on the nightingale.

The year 1922 is a landmark in modern literature, and in our special area, because it brought forth two works which, in their different ways and media, signally and radically exemplify the modern treatment of myth, in both the broad and the nar-

---

[60]F. O. Matthiessen would not allow that, here and in other poems, Eliot is setting a debased present below a great past (*The Achievement of T. S. Eliot* (3rd ed., New York, 1958), pp. 129, 39, 49, 138); but, granted Eliot's infinite subtlety of implication, it seems to me that the idea of contrast is much stronger than the idea of equation; *cf.* n. 56 above. G. Smith (p. 47), like Matthiessen, sees Agamemnon and Sweeney as cast in the same mold. Alan Holder (*Three Voyagers in Search of Europe: A Study of Henry James, Ezra Pound, and T. S. Eliot* (Philadelphia, 1966), pp. 250-252) sees Eliot's habitual contrasts as condemnations of the present, and cites the explicit conviction of modern "decline . . . in every department of human activity" (*Notes towards the Definition of Culture* (London, Faber, 1948), p. 19; (New York, Harcourt, Brace, 1949), p. 17). Holder goes on to qualify his view by reference to Eliot's Christian judgment of both past and present. D. E. S. Maxwell (p. 86: n. 58 above) takes the allusion to the Convent to represent "a distortion of values," since withdrawal from the world is not coping with it; I cannot see this.

Some possible suggestions for the opening lines of *Sweeney Among the Nightingales* may not have got into the record (though the number of books, articles, and notes forbids any confidence). In *The Works of Christopher Marlowe*, ed. Tucker Brooke (Oxford, 1910), *cf.* "gloomie Orion" (*Dido* I. ii. 274: noted by R. G. Collingwood, *The Principles of Art* (Oxford, 1938), p. 311 n.); "Now that the gloomy shadow of the earth,/Longing to view Orions drisling looke" (*Doctor Faustus*, lines 235-236); "From the bright circle of the horned Moone" (*ibid.*, p. 197, line 833) —although the horned moon was an Elizabethan commonplace. With "the Dog" *cf.* Aeschylus, *Agamemnon*, line 967, and Beaumont and Fletcher, *The Maid's Tragedy* IV. i. 55-56: "The burnt air, when the Dog reigns, is not fouler/Than thy contagious name." References to eagles and a raven as birds of prey and vengeance occur in *Agamemnon* at lines 47 f., 114-138, 1473 (Bush, *Romantic Tradition*, p. 513, n. 56). G. Smith (pp. 45-46) says that Eliot brought in the nightingales (and the bloody wood) from *Oedipus at Colonus*, but, although they are associated especially with that play, Aeschylus' chorus and Cassandra both allude to the nightingale in relevant terms (*Agam.* 1142-1148). H. Howarth (*Notes on Some Figures Behind T. S. Eliot* (Boston, 1964), p. 314) follows Smith but quotes (174) a sentence from Henri Franck about a nightingale singing near a café. For the gate of horn see Homer, *Od.* xix. 562-567, Virgil, *Aen.* vi. 893-896.

G. Jones (p. 227, n.: see n. 52 above) surely goes beyond evidence and critical wisdom in identifying all the persons of the poem with Aeschylean counterparts: Rachel and Clytemnestra, the man in mocha brown with "the redeemer-Orestes," and so on.

row sense of the word. These two epics in prose and verse, *Ulysses* and *The Waste Land,* both use heroic myth in picturing modern civilization as unheroic or antiheroic (though such labels need to be qualified). In a review in 1923 Eliot saluted Joyce for achieving a new "mythical method" for the writer facing "the immense panorama of futility and anarchy which is contemporary history"; Joyce, he said, had the power of manipulating through myth "a continuous parallel between contemporaneity and antiquity"[61]—a method and a power Eliot himself had displayed. In *Ulysses* heroic and beautiful episodes in the *Odyssey* are reduced to drab or sensual or pathetic episodes in the lives of Leopold and Molly Bloom and their fellow Dubliners—though such contrasts are somewhat mitigated by the total experience and character of the protagonist. The interwoven mythic patterns of Eliot's small but massive mosaic contrast the real and the spurious, life and sterility, love and sex, faith and emptiness.[62]

One minute but typical item is the transmutation of the "naive" freshness of Elizabethan mythologizing (in lines from John Day):

> When of the sudden, listening, you shall hear
> A noise of horns and hunting, which shall bring
> Actaeon to Diana in the spring. . . .

This springtime vision is urbanized and mechanized, with an added ironical echo of Marvell, into a travesty of love and the renewal of life:

61T. S. Eliot, *The Dial* 75 (1923) : pp. 480-483: quoted by various critics. Instead of naming a few items from the huge bibliography on Joyce's *Ulysses,* I may refer to a succinct account which comes at the end of a long story (and which gives some references), W. B. Stanford, *The Ulysses Theme* (below, Bibliography, General), pp. 211-225. Stanford notes (pp. 3, 186-187, 213, 246) that Joyce as a boy was first attracted to the story by the "mysticism" or semiallegorical quality of Charles Lamb's *Adventures of Ulysses* (1808). Helen Gardner draws an incisive contrast between *Ulysses* and *The Waste Land* (*The Art of T. S. Eliot* (New York, 1959) , pp. 84-88). *Cf.* T. M. Lorch, "The Relationship between *Ulysses* and *The Waste Land,*" *Texas Studies in Literature and Language* 6 (1964-1965) : pp. 123-133.

62Although echoes of Tennyson in Eliot have been noted by various commentators, I may throw in one that has perhaps not been recorded: with "A heap of broken images" (*Waste Land* 22) *cf.* Tennyson: " 'Heaven opens inward, chasms yawn,/Vast images in glimmering dawn,/Half shown, are broken and withdrawn' " (*The Two Voices,* lines 304-306) .

But at my back from time to time I hear
The sound of horns and motors, which shall bring
Sweeney to Mrs. Porter in the spring.[63]

In the section called "A Game of Chess" a woman who represents neurotic, loveless, meaningless existence is characterized through a luxuriant description of the jewels and synthetic perfumes on her dressing table—as Milton's fallen angels are characterized through a description of the over-rich palace they build in hell.[64] At the end—with an echo of Milton's picture of Eden as Satan enters it—we have this:

Above the antique mantel was displayed
As though a window gave upon the sylvan scene
The change of Philomel, by the barbarous king
So rudely forced; yet there the nightingale
Filled all the desert with inviolable voice
And still she cried, and still the world pursues,
"Jug Jug" to dirty ears.

The Ovidian story of Tereus' rape of Philomela is given a slightly archaic tinge because it comes by way of *Titus Andronicus*[65] and because it uses the common Elizabethan rendering of the nightingale's notes as "Jug Jug." Although this bird seems far from the nightingales singing near the Convent

---

[63]*Waste Land* iii. 196-198; and Eliot's note on John Day's *Parliament of Bees (Nero & Other Plays*, ed. H. P. Horne *et al.* (Mermaid Series, London, 1888) , p. 226) .

[64]Cf. *Paradise Lost* i. 710 f. The description that opens "A Game of Chess" seems to bear some resemblance to the opening of chapter 24 of James's *The Wings of the Dove*. In addition to the references for these lines in Eliot's notes *(Antony and Cleopatra* II. i. 190; Virgil, *Aen.* i. 726; *Paradise Lost* iv. 140; Ovid, *Metam.* iv. 424-674) , G. Melchiori finds resemblances to *Cymbeline*, Keats's *Lamia*, Joyce's *Ulysses*, and Swinburne's prose ("Echoes in 'The Waste Land,' " *English Studies* 32 (1951) : pp. 1-11, 160-161: *The Tightrope Walkers* (London, 1956) , pp. 63-88). See also G. Smith (n. 52 above) , pp. 79-83, and, for further echoes in *The Waste Land* and other poems, Irène Simon, *English Studies* 34 (1953) : pp. 64-72, and D. J. DeLaura, *English Language Notes* 3 (1965-1966) : pp. 211-221.

[65]Cf. *Titus Andronicus* IV. i. 52-53: "Ravish'd and wrong'd as Philomela was,/Forc'd in the ruthless, vast, and gloomy woods"; and "forc'd" again at V. ii. 178. For "withered stumps of time" *(Waste Land*, line 104) , *cf.* the allusions to Lavinia's "stumps" in II. iv. 4, III. ii. 42, V. ii. 183.
Cleanth Brooks, in his full analysis of *The Waste Land (Modern Poetry and the Tradition* (Chapel Hill, 1939) , p. 147; *T. S. Eliot: A Selected Critique*, ed. L. Unger (New York, 1948) , pp. 328-329) , sees Philomela as "one of the major symbols of the poem" and rape as suggesting the process of scientific secularization that has created the waste land.

of the Sacred Heart, it is not wholly dissimilar. Critics have observed the effect of the change of tense,[66] from "Filled" and "cried" to "and still the world pursues"—a change which suddenly brings the violent defiling of innocence and beauty, the translation of suffering into song, out of the mythic past into the still ugly present. We may think of Milton's allusions in *Lycidas* and *Paradise Lost* to the violent death of Orpheus and the fate of the poet in a hostile world.[67]

Among the sources Eliot mentioned in his notes are *The Golden Bough* and Ovid's *Metamorphoses*. From the latter came Tiresias,[68] the blind seer of Thebes, who had been both man and woman, had known all experience, as it were, and who, though a mere spectator, is "the most important personage in the poem, uniting all the rest. . . . What Tiresias *sees*, in fact, is the substance of the poem." Thus Tiresias, who has "foresuffered all," is akin to the prophetess Moneta in Keats's *Fall of Hyperion*. But Eliot is not, like Keats, accepting a tragic vision of the world with the purely human compassion of a naturalistic imagination. He is not, like Yeats, either celebrating fullness of heroic and sensual life or craving release from it. Nor is he, like Prufrock, merely suffering from timorous inhibitions; and water now symbolizes a far richer kind of fulfillment. In *The Waste Land* it is the Christian—and Buddhist—ideal that gives a quiet intensity of horror to the pictures of unthinking, unfeeling corruption, spiritual sickness and death. The perfunctory sexual encounter of the clerk and the typist leads on to St. Augustine's agonized memory of the fire of lust; the death of pagan gods is linked with Christ in Gethsemane; and the poem ends with the Hindu equivalent of "The

---

66The change of tense and its significance were perhaps first pointed out by Edmund Wilson (*Axel's Castle*, p. 109). In *Paradise Lost* i. 492-502 Milton, by a similar change of tense, links Belial with the corrupt clergy and upper-class hoodlums of Restoration London.

67Milton's lines on Orpheus (*P. L.* vii. 32-39) are quoted above, toward the end of I.

68"But the roots of Eliot's Tiresias include at least Sophocles, Tennyson, Swinburne, and Apollinaire, as well as the Ovid Eliot himself cites" (F. N. Lees, "Mr. Eliot's Sunday Morning *Satura:* Petronius and *The Waste Land,*" *Sewanee Review* 74 (1966) : p. 344).

Peace which passeth understanding"—although peace is still
to be attained.

In his later poems of religious meditation Eliot carried on
his magical power of word and rhythm and something of his
mythic method, but he naturally avoided mythological reference. (His dramatic adaptations of some Greek tragedies we
cannot go into.) One exception must be noted, the allusion
in the final lyric of *Little Gidding* to the poisoned robe, woven
by Hercules' loving wife, which burned him to death (we
observed before the allusions in Spenser, Shakespeare, and
Milton).[69] Eliot transposes the myth to the religious plane,
fusing together the fire from a bomber and the fires of sin and
of purifying grace:

> Who then devised the torment? Love.
> Love is the unfamiliar Name
> Behind the hands that wove
> The intolerable shirt of flame
> Which human power cannot remove.
> We only live, only suspire
> Consumed by either fire or fire.

Thus, beginning with *Prufrock*, Eliot's mythological allusions
chart a course from mildly Dionysian rebellion to wholly
Christian surrender.

Ezra Pound, the tireless crusader for "pure poetry" and modern techniques, has been commonly credited with strong influence on the early Yeats and Eliot as well as many lesser poets,
though perhaps these two original masters would, on their own,
have developed much as they did.[70] Pound was certainly a great

---

69*Little Gidding,* end of section iv. The allusions in Spenser, Shakespeare, and
Milton are noted above in I: *Faerie Queene* I. xi. 27; *Antony and Cleopatra*
IV. xii. 43 f.; *Paradise Lost* ii. 542 f. Shelley put an allusion into the curse
originally pronounced by Prometheus upon Jupiter: "Till thine Infinity shall
be/A robe of envenomed agony" *(Prometheus Unbound* I. 288-289) .

70In *The Influence of Ezra Pound* (London, 1966) , the only full and close
study, K. L. Goodwin modifies the large estimates of Pound's influence (on
Yeats, Eliot, *et al.)* that have been current for many years. *Cf.* T. Parkinson,
"Yeats and Pound: the Illusion of Influence," *CL* 6 (1954) : pp. 256-264; and
the fourth chapter of R. Ellmann's *Eminent Domain* (New York, 1967) . Pound
himself said of Eliot in 1914: "He has actually trained himself *and* modernized
himself *on his own" (The Letters of Ezra Pound 1907-1941,* ed. D. D. Paige
(New York, Harcourt, Brace and Company, 1950) , p. 40) .

energizing and astringent force in poetry; he insisted on the presentation of images and sensations with hard, clear-cut objectivity and without discursive abstractions, in colloquial, concise, concrete language. But, apart from urgent expression of his own views of poetry and culture, Pound—like that earlier technician, Landor—had not a great deal to say. He was a craftsman who outgrew the Pre-Raphaelite idiom but not very often, or very profitably, the gospel of art for art's sake.[71]

Homage to Sextus Propertius (1917: printed in 1919) was partly a making over of the Roman amorist in the modern poet's image. Pound's avowed intention was, through free reworking of Propertius, to set forth "the infinite and ineffable imbecility of the British Empire" in 1917, as a parallel to the Roman poet's view of the Roman. But the parallel was hardly valid, Pound's comprehension of public affairs could be childish or worse, and the *Homage* is really an elaborate proclamation of the aesthetic creed.[72] The much-debated *Homage* led on to the much-praised *Hugh Selwyn Mauberley* (1920), in which Pound glorified the artist and damned a cheap and tawdry civilization ("an old bitch gone in the teeth"); we might be more fully sympathetic if the voice were not that of a self-applauding, self-pitying aesthete. On the model of Gautier (and Swinburne)—and in clipped statements remote from

---

71Accounts of Pound's non-literary interests and activities are given in, e.g., Charles Norman, *Ezra Pound* (New York, Macmillan, 1960), and Noel Stock, *Poet in Exile: Ezra Pound* (Manchester, 1964).

72Pound said emphatically that the *Homage* was not offered as a translation (*Letters*, pp. 148-149; Norman, *Ezra Pound* (1960), pp. 205-207), but it has often been condemned as if it were. The fullest and best account of the poem is J. P. Sullivan's *Ezra Pound and Sextus Propertius: A Study in Creative Translation* (Austin, 1964); cf. Sullivan, "Pound and Propertius: Some Techniques of Translation," *Hereditas*, ed. Frederic Will (Austin, 1964), pp. 97-119. Propertius was much more addicted to mythology than the other Roman amorists, and Pound reduced that element (Sullivan, pp. 44-46); there is a similar reduction in Robert Lowell's notable *The Ghost (After Sextus Propertius)*, as Sullivan observes in reprinting it (pp. 180-183).

For the topical strain in the *Homage* see Pound's *Letters*, p. 231; for the same in the *Cantos*, ibid., pp. 191, 239. See Sullivan, especially pp. 36, 58-64, 75-76. Donald Davie *(Ezra Pound: Poet as Sculptor* (New York, 1964), p. 85) affirms that the *Homage* "is in the fullest sense an occasional poem" and is "written against imperialism and against war." Is that the total effect of the poem upon a disinterested reader?

Yeats's lyric eloquence—Pound describes Dionysian sensuality
as conquered by Christian asceticism; and, though in fact a
contemptuous anti-Christian, he goes on, with dubious sincerity, to find further evidence of modern decay in the loss of
the saint's vision and the sacred wafer.[73]

Pound's voluminous *Cantos* should claim our prolonged
attention because of his devotion to Ovid and his framework
of myth and metamorphosis and many details; however, I lack
both time and the requisite discernment. Pound's theme, said
Yeats, is flux,[74] and his mythic method is that of *The Waste
Land*, but Eliot's rendering of flux, for all its elliptical
complexities, makes a potent and poignant impact upon even
a half-informed reader. Whether *The Waste Land* gained or
lost under the slashing Pound's "desp'rate hook,"[75] the weapon
was not applied to the garrulity and pedantry of the *Cantos*.
These have their stirring passages: one is the opening, on
Odysseus' descent to Hades, paraphrased in the style of Pound's
Seafarer. But, for the work as a whole, one may cite Yeats again,
though this judgment was made before the poem had reached its
full length: while Yeats found "heroic sincerity" in the *Cantos*
and in Joyce's *Anna Livia Plurabelle*, he saw both works—in

73The phrase from *Hugh Selwyn Mauberley* is quoted from *Personae: The
Collected Poems of Ezra Pound* (New York, New Directions, (1949), p. 191,
and *Selected Poems of Ezra Pound (ibid.*, 1957), p. 64. Gautier's lines (quoted
above in n. 7) are quoted in the fullest account of the poem, John J. Espey,
Ezra Pound's Mauberley: A Study in Composition (Berkeley and London, 1955),
p. 36; Espey notes that Pound's "macerations" *(Mauberley* iii) may come from
the preface to Gautier's *Mademoiselle de Maupin*. See also the analysis in M. L.
Rosenthal, *A Primer of Ezra Pound* (New York, 1960), pp. 29-41.

74W. B. Yeats, *Oxford Book Of Modern Verse* (1936), p. xxiv; see also *A
Vision* (New York, 1962), pp. 4-5, and Pound's own fuller summary of 1927
(Letters, pp. 210-211). The plan of the *Cantos* is set forth in Sister M. Bernetta
Quinn's *The Metamorphic Tradition in Modern Poetry* (New Brunswick,
1955), pp. 14-48, and in the multiplying books on Pound and on the poem.
Following Pound's own division of his material into "the permanent, the
recurrent, the casual" *(Letters,* p. 239), E. M. Glenn explained the "permanent"
level of being as represented by the gods, such as Aphrodite, the "recurrent"
by such archetypal figures, mythological or historical, as Odysseus, Helen, *et al.*
("A Guide to *Canto II* of Ezra Pound," *The Analyst* 18 (Northwestern University, n.d.) : pp. 3-4: quoted by Alan Holder, *Three Voyagers* (n. 60 above),
p. 229.

75T. S. Eliot ("Ezra Pound," *New English Weekly* 30 (1946): pp. 27-28;
Poetry 68 (1946) : p. 330) said that Pound cut *The Waste Land* down to about
half its original length.

contrast to "The romantic movement with its turbulent heroism, its self-assertion"—as examples of "a new naturalism that leaves man helpless before the contents of his own mind."[76] Yvor Winters, that resolute nay-sayer, succinctly labeled Pound "a sensibility without a mind."[77] Of course Pound's devoted exegetes reject or ignore such blasphemies.

If, like Pound, we could go on indefinitely, we should take in a number of other poets, such as the "pagan" D. H. Lawrence or Robert Graves, who carry into poetry their common though very different concern with love and with mythology; but our main theme suggests a deeply, quietly reflective writer of another stamp. The self-taught, isolated Edwin Muir (1887-1959) surmounted much harsh experience, and came late to poetry, later still to an undogmatic Christian faith.[78] His earliest sense, in the Orkney Islands, of having "one foot in Eden," his serious interest in dreams, and his and his wife's translating of Kafka are partial clues to his ethical, metaphysical, and increasingly religious preoccupation with time and eternity, guilt and grace, and to the mythic or visionary form and atmosphere of poems detached from contemporary imme-

[76]Yeats, "Bishop Berkeley" (1931), in *Essays and Introductions* (New York, Macmillan, 1961), p. 405.

[77]Yvor Winters, *The Anatomy of Nonsense* (Norfolk, Conn., New Directions, 1943), p. 161; p. 496 in *In Defense of Reason* (Denver, Alan Swallow, n.d.).

[78]Most of the better critical studies of Edwin Muir have been done since his death—and are marked by a tone of something more than respect for both the man and the poet which is unusual in modern criticism. Some of these are: R. P. Blackmur, *Kenyon Review* 21 (1959): pp. 419-436, repr. in *Four Poets on Poetry*, ed. Don C. Allen (Baltimore, 1959); P. H. Butter, *Edwin Muir: Man and Poet* (Edinburgh and London, 1966; New York, 1967); Helen Gardner, *Edwin Muir*, a lecture (Cardiff, 1961); Ada Giaccari, *English Miscellany* 15 (1964): pp. 259-312; J. C. Hall, *Edwin Muir* (British Council Pamphlet No. 71, 1956); M. Hamburger, *Encounter* 15, 6 (1960): pp. 46-53; I. H. Hassan, *South Atlantic Quarterly* 58 (1959): pp. 427-439; Daniel Hoffman, *Barbarous Knowledge: Myth in the Poetry of Yeats, Graves, and Muir* (New York, 1967); John Holloway, *Hudson Review* 13 (1960-1961): pp. 550-567, an essay of special interest in regard to the classical poems; Elizabeth Jennings, *London Magazine* 7, 3 (1960): pp. 43-56; R. J. Mills, *Accent* 19 (1959): pp. 50-70, and *The Personalist* 44 (1963), pp. 58-78; Kathleen Raine, *Texas Quarterly* 4, 3 (1961): pp. 233-245; J. H. Summers, *Massachusetts Review* 2 (1960-1961): pp. 240-260; J. R. Watson, *Critical Quarterly* 6 (1964): pp. 231-249. E. G. Mellown's *Bibliography of the Writings of Edwin Muir* (London, 1966) includes a selected list of critiques. I have used *Edwin Muir: Collected Poems* (London, Faber; New York, Oxford University Press, 1965).

diacy and contemporary poetics. For Muir as for many other poets classical myths were a means of objectifying personal experience: *Orpheus' Dream* is no less moving a poem of love than the direct *Confirmation*. As a boy Muir had delighted especially in a book of selections from Morris' *Earthly Paradise*;[79] but the poet far outgrew Morris in his visions of paradise and earth and evil. Some of his most penetrating comments on Hölderlin make one think of his own poetry.[80]

From Virgil through variations on the medieval formula *Ubi sunt* on up to our own day, fallen Troy and long-dead heroes and Helen have evoked reflections on the pathos of destructive time. Muir's Trojan poems have little or nothing of Yeats's epic and prophetic splendor; they link the passage of time with the realities of experience and common human feelings, somewhat distanced and philosophized. In boyhood Muir associated Troy with a green mound near his father's house; and the fine early *Ballad of Hector in Hades*, in which Hector re-enacts his flight from Achilles, was a "resuscitation" of the "real terror" the poet had felt as a boy when he fled from a schoolfellow.[81] In *Troy*, an offbeat and grimly ironic postscript to "Proud history," a mad old man, fighting rats as he hunts for scraps in the sewers of the abandoned city, thinks he is battling the Greeks; at last he is dragged to the surface and tortured to death by robbers who suspect he knows of buried treasure.[82] The poems as collected in 1952 included three called *The Return* (one on Ulysses and Penelope, another on the Greeks' coming back from Troy), and the repeated title suggests Muir's abiding sense of continuity and change in the individual life

---

79Muir, *Autobiography* (London, Hogarth Press, 1954), p. 77.

80"Friedrich Hölderlin," "Hölderlin's *Patmos*," in *Essays on Literature and Society*, revised and enlarged edition (London, Hogarth Press, 1965).

81On the *Ballad of Hector* see Muir, *Autobiography*, pp. 42-43, 206. D. Hoffman (*Barbarous Knowledge*, pp. 247-256: n. 78 above) comments on Muir's Trojan poems, on his "themes of mortal defeat and predestined journey," on his implicit linking of Troy with Scotland (*cf.* Muir's *Scottish Journey*, on Scotland in the depression), and especially on the soul's journey through the life-long labyrinth and its "return to the sacred place from which our life began."

82On *Troy*, see Holloway, pp. 561-562 (n. 78 above). In this poem K. L. Goodwin (*Influence of Ezra Pound*, pp. 211-212: n. 70 above) sees marks of Pound's narrative style and cites in particular the beginning of *Canto iv*.

and that life's repetition of the life of man; with these pieces may be linked the more richly charged *Telemachos Remembers*.[83] In various Biblical and mythological poems, set in a perspective of time and memory, the theme of return and reconciliation, of loss and recovery, overcomes the legacy of Adam. The insoluble mysteries of life and evil remain mysteries, but affirmations are still possible—though they may differ in poetic validity. Muir's Prometheus, at the world's end, will not get an answer from Olympus (perhaps then vacant), but will if he can find the god who came down from another heaven "Not in rebellion but in pity and love."[84] Although for Muir—as for Eliot—the Incarnation had become the central fact and mystery of life, this conclusion of a strong poem may seem unwontedly pat; *The Grave of Prometheus* is more inconclusive and more impressive. Muir's Prometheus is obviously not Byronic or Shelleyan; nor, though the poet had once clung passionately to Nietzsche, does he partake of what Erich Heller terms "The all-engulfing weariness of a Nietzschean Prometheus."[85]

Two poems that stress the difficult recognition of a divine order in life are *Oedipus* and *The Labyrinth*. In the first the aged sufferer feels that he has been led by the gods from his early marriage and patricide, from unwitting guilt and fear, to the peace of something like divine insight into the universal sharing of wrong.[86] *The Labyrinth*—which only touches Theseus and the Minotaur—is an inner debate between nihil-

---

83On *The Return of Odysseus* (the 1965 title) and *Telemachos Remembers* see Holloway, pp. 554-557, and Butter, pp. 253-254 (both listed in n. 78 above); on *Penelope in Doubt*, Butter, pp. 288-289. On the repetition in the individual life of the life of man, see *Autobiography*, p. 49; *The Estate of Poetry* (Cambridge, Mass., 1962), pp. 87-88.

84*Prometheus* (1954) was offered in response to T. S. Eliot's request for a poem to be included in Faber's Ariel series. Butter (p. 252) quotes a letter in which Eliot, while praising the poem, asked if the author could iron out the difficulty of having Prometheus survive into our own epoch.

85Erich Heller (*The Disinherited Mind*, p. 163: n. 32 above) quoted the fourth of Kafka's Prometheus legends: "Everyone grew weary of the meaningless affair. The gods grew weary, the eagles grew weary, the wound closed wearily." (Kafka, *The Great Wall of China*, tr. Willa and Edwin Muir (London, 1946), p. 129; (New York, 1946), p. 251).

86In a later and shorter poem, *The Other Oedipus* (*Collected Poems* (London, 1965), p. 217), the aged sufferer has become gay and innocent because his mind is gone and he has clean forgotten "That memory burning in another world."

ism and faith somewhat akin to Tennyson's *Two Voices*. The speaker could not live unless convinced that "the endless maze" of life and time and self is illusion, that there are gods in an "eternal dialogue" of peace; in that "real world"

> all these things were woven; and this our life
> Was as a chord deep in that dialogue—

but a brief summary of the conclusion is more facile than the poem.[87] Muir's religious vision of good is valid because it has to conquer a potent vision of evil. Milton, he says (in his late sonnet *Milton*), had

> heard the steely clamour known too well
> On Saturday nights in every street in Hell.
> Where, past the devilish din, could Paradise be?
> A footstep more, and his unblinded eyes
> Saw far and near the fields of Paradise.

The last line and a half are fittingly inscribed on Muir's gravestone.

The sketch of our century, as of earlier centuries, has been only a sketch. Both Renaissance and Romantic poets could combine serious idealism with sensuous luxuriance, but the climate and temper of our time forbid that. Modern mythological poems, or incidental references or bare titles, are likely to be ironic, disillusioned comments on unheroic and ugly aspects of our world: one example is Auden's *The Shield of Achilles*. Of course many modern poets have used mythology sparsely or not at all; Americans in the Whitman tradition have mainly followed the master's precept and practice (the great American mythic poem, in part a Promethean re-creation, is *Moby Dick*). While the use of mythology has lessened, we have had fresh and strong translations of ancient poems and plays from a number of scholarly poets, Richmond Lattimore,

---

[87]Butter (pp. 215-216) quotes Muir's statements about his taking the Labyrinth as "an image of human life with its errors and ignorance and endless intricacy" (the first sentence of the poem being "deliberately labyrinthine"), and also about his wish "to give an image of the life of the gods, to whom all that is confusion down here is clear and harmonious as seen eternally." Butter takes the poem as in part, but only in part, autobiography.

Robert Fitzgerald, Dudley Fitts, and others. The word "translation" is inadequate for Robert Lowell's prose version of the Aeschylean *Prometheus*, which works modern variations on the problems of consciousness and power, on the text that "intelligence is suffering." The summer of 1967 also brought a wholly original drama, the *Herakles* of Archibald MacLeish: here the linking of a modern physicist with the Greek hero presents a parallel of triumphant achievement and disastrous futility.[88] The Christian assurance that Edwin Muir attached to the myths of Prometheus and the Labyrinth is not in these plays, which are much more typical of our time: MacLeish's scientist has threaded the labyrinth, but, like the ancient Theseus, has fatally forgotten his human ties.

If we look back over the whole story, recognizing the profound changes in man's outer and inner worlds, some elements of change and continuity are clear. Although the failure of communication among specialized groups is a cliché of modern culture, classical mythology is still something of a general possession; college students readily distinguish Orpheus from Oedipus—though they may confuse Abraham with Absalom and Joshua with Judas. If myth is not now the staple currency it was in most earlier ages, it has furnished memorable images and symbols for the two greatest modern poets in English and for a number of lesser ones. The reason is not merely literary tradition but the instinctive sense, so urgent in modern times, that myth belongs to man's natural and imaginative being and is a unique resource in a world of intellectual abstractions, technological power, and contempt for the past.

In poetry from the Renaissance onward, the ethical and the naturalistic conceptions of classical myth have co-existed (and, however different poets' intentions, there has been no necessary difference in the manner of artistic treatment). The ethical attitude has commonly predominated, though it has more and more lost its old Christian connection and support; but the ideal or archetypal character of myth has remained vital, since it is the *sine qua non*. And although the general modern out-

---

[88]For Lowell and MacLeish, see above, Preface, note 7.

look is more rationalistic than religious, it has still been possible for Christian poets like Eliot and Muir to carry on, with sophisticated sincerity, the old tradition of Christian assimilation of pagan myth.[89] It has also been possible for the non-Christian Yeats to weave mythology into a visionary supernaturalism hardly less repugnant to skeptical reason.[90] It may be that these "were the last romantics,"[91] and that poetry is to follow William Carlos Williams' principle, "No ideas but in things,"[92] or Wallace Stevens' richer concern with fact, with reality and imagination. (And Stevens himself could pay tribute to the tradition, most notably in the late and fine poem on Penelope and Ulysses called *The World as Meditation*[93]—

---

[89]In recent years a good many books have described both a resurgence of more or less reinterpreted Christianity in a number of modern Christian writers and varying approximations to a religious view of good and evil in a number of uncommitted or even anti-Christian ones. Some of these are books written or edited by Cleanth Brooks, Charles I. Glicksberg, Stanley R. Hopper, Kathleen E. Morgan, William R. Mueller, W. T. Noon, Nathan A. Scott (who has been especially active), W. V. Spanos, Martin Turnell, Amos N. Wilder. The latest volumes that I have seen are Frederick J. Hoffman's *The Imagination's New Beginning: Theology and Modern Literature* (Notre Dame, 1967) and *Mansions of the Spirit: Essays in Religion and Literature*, ed. G. A. Panichas (New York, 1967). See also *Literature and Belief: English Institute Essays 1957*, ed. M. H. Abrams (New York, 1958).

Some historical surveys of English poetry and religion, of varying scope and size, are listed below in the Bibliography, General: see H. N. Fairchild, Roland M. Frye, E. Jennings, A. S. P. Woodhouse. One may add J. Hillis Miller, *The Disappearance of God: Five Nineteenth-Century Writers* (Cambridge, Mass., 1963) and Robert M. Adams, *Nil: Episodes in the literary conquest of void during the nineteenth century* (New York, 1966).

[90]This general theme comes up more or less in all the books on Yeats: see, e.g., Alex Zwerdling, *Yeats and the Heroic Ideal* (1965), p. 156 (and pp. 132-178).

[91]Yeats, *Coole Park and Ballylee, 1931 (C.P.,* p. 240).

[92]The maxim "No ideas but in things" appeared in *The Autobiography of William Carlos Williams* (New York, Random House, 1951), p. 390. Williams, while a medical student, worshiped Keats, and wrote a long poem on the model of *Endymion (ibid.,* pp. 53, 59-61).

[93]For comments on *The World as Meditation (Collected Poems* (New York, Knopf, 1955), pp. 520-521), see, e.g., F. Kermode, *Wallace Stevens* (Edinburgh and London, 1960), pp. 92, 123-124; J. J. Enck, *Wallace Stevens* (Carbondale, 1964), p. 193; Louis L. Martz, *The Poem of Mind* (New York, 1966), pp. 200-202, 218-220. Along with occasional mythological allusions, there is also Stevens' *The Sail of Ulysses (Opus Posthumous,* ed. S. F. Morse (New York, Knopf, 1957), pp. 99-105), a poem read at the Phi Beta Kappa exercises at Columbia University in 1954. His "Adagia" include this item: "The greatest piece of fiction: Greek mythology. Classical mythology but Greek above Latin" *(ibid.,* p. 178).

which is both like and unlike Edwin Muir's more homely and Homeric meditations on the theme.) At any rate, in a world so much committed to the subhuman, we may hope that classical myth will continue its long life as a symbolic language of human and superhuman vision.

Bibliography*

GENERAL

AGARD, WALTER R. 1951. *Classical Myths in Sculpture* (Madison) .

BOLGAR, R. R. 1954. *The Classical Heritage and Its Beneficiaries.* (Cambridge) .

BREWER, WILMON. 1933-1957. *Ovid's Metamorphoses in European Culture* (3 v., Boston and Francestown, N.H.) .

CASTELAIN, M. July 1932. "Démogorgon ou le barbarisme déifié." *Bulletin de l'association Guillaume Budé,* No. 36: pp. 22-39.

COCHRANE, CHARLES N. 1944. *Christianity and Classical Culture: A Study of Thought and Action from Augustus to Augustine.* (London) .

CRUMP, M. M. 1931. *The Epyllion from Theocritus to Ovid* (Oxford) .

EDELSTEIN, L. 1953. "The Golden Chain of Homer." *Studies in Intellectual History* (Baltimore) , pp. 48-66.

FAIRCHILD, HOXIE N. 1939-1962. *Religious Trends in English Poetry.* 6 v. Vols. 1-5 (1700-1920) , New York.

FINSLER, GEORG. 1912. *Homer in der Neuzeit von Dante bis Goethe* (Leipzig and Berlin) .

FRYE, NORTHROP. 1947. *Anatomy of Criticism* (Princeton) .

FRYE, ROLAND M. 1961. *Perspective on Man: Literature and the Christian Tradition* (Philadelphia) .

GRANT, MICHAEL. 1962. *Myths of the Greeks and Romans* (London) .

GUTHRIE, W. K. C. 1950-1951. *The Greeks and Their Gods* (London; Boston) .

HEINEMANN, KARL. 1920. *Die tragischen Gestalten der Griechen in der Weltliteratur* (2 v. Leipzig) .

HIGHET, GILBERT. 1949. *The Classical Tradition: Greek and Roman Influences on Western Literature* (New York and London) .

HINKS, ROGER. 1939. *Myth and Allegory in Ancient Art* (London) .

HOFFMANN, ADOLF. 1908. *Das Psyche-Märchen des Apuleius in der englischen Literatur* (Strassburg) .

JENNINGS, ELIZABETH. 1965. *Christian Poetry* (London and New York) .

Larousse Encyclopedia of Mythology (New York, 1959) .

LAVIN, IRVING. 1954. "Cephalus and Procris: Transformations of an Ovidian Myth." *JWCI* 17: pp. 260-287.

LAW, HELEN H. 1932. *Bibliography of Greek Myth in English Poetry.* New York: American Classical League Service Bureau, Bulletin 27; *Supplement* (1941) .

LeCOMTE, EDWARD S. 1944. *Endymion in England: The Literary History of A Greek Myth* (New York) .

---

* This very limited bibliography (which has one general section and three **o**ther sections corresponding to the three lectures) lists only a fraction of the scholarly and critical writings cited above in the notes. It includes mainly studies in the mythological and the classical tradition that have not been already cited. Much fuller bibliographies are given in my two volumes (see sections I and II below), although the one on the Romantic tradition (1937) is obviously out of date. In the present book bibliographical notes on individual poets and myths may be found through the index.

MALRAUX, ANDRÉ. 1960. *The Metamorphosis of the Gods*, tr. Stuart Gilbert (New York).

MERIVALE, PATRICIA. 1969. *Pan the Goat-God* (Cambridge, Mass.).

MUSURILLO, HERBERT. 1961. *Symbol and Myth in Ancient Poetry* (New York).

OTIS, BROOKS. 1966. *Ovid as an Epic Poet* (Cambridge).

PANOFSKY, DORA and ERWIN. 1956. *Pandora's Box: The Changing Aspects of a Mythical Symbol* (New York; 2nd ed., 1962).

PANOFSKY, ERWIN. 1930. *Hercules am Scheidewege und Andere Antike Bildstoffe in der Neueren Kunst.* Studien der Bibliothek Warburg 18 (Leipzig-Berlin).

RAGGIO, OLGA. 1958. "The Myth of Prometheus: its survival and metamorphoses up to the eighteenth century." *JWCI* 21: pp. 44-62.

RAHNER, HUGO. 1963. *Greek Myths and Christian Mystery*, tr. B. Battershaw (London and New York).

RAND, EDWARD K. 1925. *Ovid and his Influence* (Boston; New York, 1928).

ROSE, HERBERT J. 1928. *Handbook of Greek Mythology including its extension to Rome* (London; 6th ed., 1958).

SANDERSON, JAMES L., et al., eds. 1966-1968. *Phaedra and Hippolytus; Medea; Oedipus; Orestes and Electra* (Boston). Each volume contains five plays on the theme and critical essays.

SCHERER, MARGARET R. 1963. *The Legends of Troy in Art and Literature* (London and New York).

SPENCER, TERENCE. 1954. *Fair Greece Sad Relic: Literary Philhellenism from Shakespeare to Byron* (London).

STANFORD, W. B. 1954. *The Ulysses Theme: A Study in the Adaptability of a Traditional Hero* (Oxford; 2nd ed., rev., 1963).

THOMSON, J. A. K. 1948. *The Classical Background of English Literature.* (London).

—— 1951. *Classical Influences on English Poetry* (London).

TROUSSON, RAYMOND. 1964. *Le Thème de Prométhée dans la littérature européenne* (2 v., Geneva).

VINGE, LOUISE. 1967. *The Narcissus Theme in Western European Literature up to the Early Nineteenth Century* (Lund).

WILKINSON, L. P. 1955. *Ovid Recalled* (Cambridge).

WOLFF, EMIL. 1947. *Die goldene Kette: Die Aurea Catena Homeri in der englischen Literatur von Chaucer bis Wordsworth* (Hamburg).

WOODHOUSE, ARTHUR S. P. 1965. *The Poet and his Faith: Religion and Poetry in England from Spenser to Eliot and Auden* (Chicago).

YOUNG, ARTHUR M. 1958. *Legend Builders of the West* (Pittsburgh).

—— 1948. *Troy and her Legend* (Pittsburgh).

I

BALDWIN, THOMAS W. 1944. *William Shakespere's Small Latine & Lesse Greeke* (2 v., Urbana).

BORN, L. K. 1934. "Ovid and Allegory." *Speculum* 9: pp. 362-379.

BRADBROOK, MURIEL C. 1951. *Shakespeare and Elizabethan Poetry* (London).

BUSH, DOUGLAS. 1932. *Mythology and the Renaissance Tradition in English Poetry* (Minneapolis; rev. ed., New York, 1963). Cited in notes as *Renaissance Tradition.*

COOKE, J. D. 1927. "Euhemerism: A Mediaeval Interpretation of Classical Paganism." *Speculum* 2: pp. 396-410.

CURRY, WALTER C. 1923. "Astrologising the Gods." *Anglia* 47: pp. 213-243.

CURTIUS, ERNST R. 1953, 1963. *European Literature and the Latin Middle Ages*, tr. W. R. Trask (New York).

DORAN, MADELEINE. 1964. "Some Renaissance 'Ovids.'" *Literature and Society,* ed. B. Slote (Lincoln, Neb.).

GIAMATTI, A. BARTLETT. 1966. *The Earthly Paradise and the Renaissance Epic* (Princeton).

GOMBRICH, E. H. 1948. "Icones Symbolicae. The Visual Image in Neo-Platonic Thought." *JWCI* 11: pp. 163-192.

GREEN, RICHARD H. 1960. "Classical Fable and English Poetry in the Fourteenth Century." *Critical Approaches to Medieval Literature,* ed. Dorothy Bethurum (New York), pp. 110-133.

GREENE, THOMAS. 1963. *The Descent from Heaven: A Study in Epic Continuity* (New Haven and London).

GRUPPE, OTTO. 1921. *Geschichte der klassischen Mythologie und Religionsgeschichte während des Mittelalters im Abendland und während der Neuzeit* (Leipzig).

HENKEL, M. D. 1930. "Illustrierte Ausgaben von Ovids Metamorphosen im XV., XVI. und XVII. Jahrhundert." *Bibliothek Warburg: Vorträge 1926-27,* pp. 58-144.

JUNG, MARC-RENÉ. 1966. *Hercule dans la littérature française du XVIe siècle: De l'Hercule courtois à l'Hercule baroque* (Geneva).

KERMODE, FRANK. 1961-1962. "The Banquet of Sense." *Bulletin of the John Rylands Library* 44: pp. 68-99.

KIMBROUGH, ROBERT. 1964. *Shakespeare's Troilus & Cressida and its Setting* (Cambridge, Mass.).

MUNARI, FRANCO. 1960. *Ovid im Mittelalter* (Zurich and Stuttgart).

PANOFSKY, ERWIN and F. SAXL. 1932-1933. "Classical Mythology in Mediaeval Art." *Metropolitan Museum Studies* 4: pp. 228-280.

PANOFSKY, ERWIN. 1960. *Renaissance and Renascences in Western Art* (Stockholm).

—— 1939. *Studies in Iconology: Humanistic Themes In the Art of the Renaissance* (New York; 2nd ed., 1962).

PRESSON, ROBERT K. 1953. *Shakespeare's Troilus and Cressida & the Legends of Troy* (Madison).

RICHMOND, H. M. 1960. "Polyphemus in England: A Study in Comparative Literature." *CL* 12: pp. 229-242.

SCHIRMER, WALTER F. 1933. *Antike, Renaissance und Puritanismus* (rev. ed., Munich).

SEZNEC, JEAN. 1953, 1961. *The Survival of the Pagan Gods,* tr. B. F. Sessions (New York).

SHAKESPEARE, WILLIAM. 1953. *Troilus and Cressida,* ed. H. N. Hillebrand and T. W. Baldwin (New Variorum Edition, Philadelphia).

SMITH, HALLETT. 1952. *Elizabethan Poetry: A Study in Conventions, Meaning, and Expression* (Cambridge, Mass.).

STARNES, DEWITT T., and E. W. TALBERT. 1955. *Classical Myth and Legend in Renaissance Dictionaries* (Chapel Hill).

SWARDSON, H. R. 1962. *Poetry and the Fountain of Light: Observations on the Conflict between Christian and Classical Traditions in Seventeenth-Century Poetry* (Columbia, Mo., and London).

TATLOCK, J. S. P. 1915. "The Siege of Troy in Elizabethan Literature." *PMLA* 30: pp. 673-770.

THOMSON, J. A. K. 1952. *Shakespeare and the Classics* (London).

TUVE, ROSEMOND. 1966. *Allegorical Imagery: Some Mediaeval Books and their Posterity* (Princeton).

WAITH, EUGENE M. 1962. *The Herculean Hero in Marlowe, Chapman, Shakespeare, & Dryden* (New York).

WALKER, D. P. 1954. "The *Prisca Theologia* in France." *JWCI* 17: pp. 204-259.

WILLIAMS, ARNOLD. 1948. *The Common Expositor: An Account of the Commentaries on Genesis 1527-1633* (Chapel Hill), chap. x, "The Classics."

WIND, EDGAR. 1958. *Pagan Mysteries in the Renaissance* (New Haven).

II

BENZIGER, JAMES. 1962. *Images of Eternity: Studies in the Poetry of Religious Vision* (Carbondale).

BLOOM, HAROLD. 1961. *The Visionary Company: A Reading of English Romantic Poetry* (New York).

—— 1961. "Napoleon and Prometheus: The Romantic Myth of Organic Energy." *Yale French Studies*, No. 26: pp. 79-82.

BROWER, R. A. 1959. *Alexander Pope: The Poetry of Allusion* (Oxford).

BUSH, DOUGLAS. 1937. *Mythology and the Romantic Tradition in English Poetry* (Cambridge, Mass.; New York, 1963). Cited in the notes as *Romantic Tradition*.

CANAT, RENÉ. 1951-1955. *L'Hellénisme des romantiques* (3 v., Paris).

DE VANE, WILLIAM C. 1940. "Browning and the Spirit of Greece." *Nineteenth-Century Studies*, ed. Herbert Davis, W. C. De Vane, and R. C. Bald (Ithaca), pp. 179-198.

FORD, GEORGE H. 1944. *Keats and the Victorians: A Study of His Influence and Rise to Fame 1821-1895* (New Haven).

FORSYTH, R. A. 1964. "The Myth of Nature and the Victorian Compromise of the Imagination." *ELH* 31: pp. 213-240.

GAY, PETER. 1966. *The Enlightenment: An Interpretation: The Rise of Modern Paganism* (New York).

GUTTELING, JOHANNA F. C. [1922]. *Hellenic Influence on the English Poetry of the Nineteenth Century* (Amsterdam).

HATFIELD, HENRY. 1964. *Aesthetic Paganism in German Literature From Winckelmann to the Death of Goethe* (Cambridge, Mass.).

HAUSER, D. R. 1966. "Pope's Lodona and the Uses of Mythology." *SEL* 6: pp. 465-482.

HELLER, J. L. 1945. "Classical Mythology in the *Systema Naturae* of Linnaeus." *Transactions of the American Philological Association* 76: pp. 333-357.

HUNGERFORD, EDWARD B. 1941. *Shores of Darkness* (New York).

JAMES, D. G. 1948. *The Romantic Comedy* (London).

KREUTZ, CHRISTIAN. 1963. *Das Prometheussymbol in der Dichtung der englischen Romantik. Palaestra* 236 (Göttingen).

KUHN, A. J. 1956. "English Deism and the Development of Romantic Mythological Syncretism." *PMLA* 71: pp. 1094-1115.

LARRABEE, STEPHEN A. 1943. *English Bards and Grecian Marbles: The Relationship between Sculpture and Poetry Especially in the Romantic Period* (New York).

LEVIN, HARRY. 1931. *The Broken Column: A Study in Romantic Hellenism* (Cambridge, Mass.).

MANUEL, FRANK E. 1959. *The Eighteenth Century Confronts the Gods* (Cambridge, Mass.).

OSBORN, JAMES M. 1963. "Travel Literature and the Rise of Neo-Hellenism in England." *Bulletin of the New York Public Library* 67: pp. 279-300.

PAPAJEWSKI, H. 1960. "Die literarische Wertung Ovids am Ausgang des 17. und zu Beginn des 18. Jahrhunderts." *Anglia* 78: pp. 422-448.

PERKINS, DAVID. 1959. *The Quest for Permanence: The Symbolism of Wordsworth Shelley and Keats* (Cambridge, Mass.).

PEYRE, HENRI. 1932. *Bibliographie critique de l'hellénisme en France de 1843 à 1870* (New Haven).

PIERCE, F. E. 1917. "The Hellenic Current in English Nineteenth Century Poetry." *JEGP* 16: pp. 103-135.

SPINDLER, ROBERT. 1930. *Robert Browning und die Antike* (Leipzig).

STERN, BERNARD H. 1940. *The Rise of Romantic Hellenism in English Literature 1732-1785* (Menasha).

STRICH, FRITZ. 1910. *Die Mythologie in der deutschen Literatur von Klopstock bis Wagner* (2 v., Halle).

TEAGARDEN, L. J. 1945-1946. "The Myth of the Hamadryad and Its Continuity." *Studies in English* (University of Texas), pp. 115-128.

TRICKETT, RACHEL. 1953. "The Augustan Pantheon: Mythology and Personification in Eighteenth-Century Poetry." *Essays and Studies 1953* (London), pp. 71-86.

WALZEL, OSKAR. 1932. *Das Prometheussymbol von Shaftesbury zu Goethe* (Munich).

ZWERDLING, ALEX. 1964. "The Mythographers and the Romantic Revival of Greek Myth." *PMLA* 79: pp. 447-456.

III

BOWRA, SIR MAURICE. 1943. *The Heritage of Symbolism* (London).

DORSON, R. M. 1955. "The Eclipse of Solar Mythology." *Journal of American Folklore* 68: pp. 393-416; repr. in *Myth: A Symposium*, ed. T. A. Sebeok (Philadelphia, 1955; Bloomington, 1958).

FRAZER, SIR JAMES G. 1890. *The Golden Bough: A Study in Comparative Religion* (2 v., London; 2nd ed., revised and enlarged, 3 v., 1900; 3rd ed., 12 v., 1907-1915).

GLÜCKSMANN, HEDWIG L. 1932. *Die Gegenüberstellung von Antike-Christentum in der englischen Literatur des 19. Jahrhunderts* (Hannover). [On Swinburne and Pater.]

HARRISON, J. S. 1924. "Pater, Heine, and the Old Gods of Greece." *PMLA* 39: pp. 655-686.

HERBERT, KEVIN. 1959-1960. "The Theseus Theme: Some Recent Versions." *Classical Journal* 55: pp. 175-185.

HOFFMAN, DANIEL. 1967. *Barbarous Knowledge: Myth in the Poetry of Yeats, Graves, and Muir* (New York).

IRWIN, W. R. 1961. "The Survival of Pan." *PMLA* 76: pp. 159-167.

KISSANE, JAMES. 1962. "Victorian Mythology." *Victorian Studies* 6: pp. 5-28.

MERIVALE, PATRICIA. 1965. "The Pan Figure in Victorian Poetry: Landor to Meredith." *Philological Quarterly* 44: pp. 258-277.

PATER, WALTER. 1876. "The Myth of Demeter and Persephone." *Fortnightly Review* 25; "A Study of Dionysus,' *ibid.* 26 (1876), and other essays, mostly collected in *Greek Studies* (1895).

QUINN, SISTER M. BERNETTA. 1955. *The Metamorphic Tradition in Modern Poetry* (New Brunswick).

VICKERY, J. B. 1956-1957. "*The Golden Bough* and Modern Poetry." *Journal of Aesthetics and Art Criticism* 15: pp. 271-288.

——— 1963. "*The Golden Bough*: Impact and Archetype." *Myth and Symbol*, ed. B. Slote (Lincoln, Neb.), repr. from *Virginia Quarterly Review* 39 (1963-1964) : pp. 36-57.

WILL, FREDERIC, ed. 1964. *Hereditas: Seven Essays on the Modern Experience of the Classical* (Austin).

Index*

Abrams, M. H., 33, 38, 97
Achilles. x, 12, 53, 57, 74, 93
Adams, Robert M., 15, 97
Adkins, S. D., 7
Adler, Joshua, 50
Adonis, 17, 27, 65, 73
Aeneas, x, 3, 19, 24
Aeschylus, x–xii, 41, 42–43, 84, 85, 96
Aestheticism, 60*
Agamemnon, xii, 76, 78, 84, 85
Alexander, Nigel, 16
Alfred, William, xii
Allegory, 2*–5*, 10–12, 14–15, 21, 26, 32
Allen, Don C., 5, 17, 22, 23, 24, 26
Allen, G. O., 47
Allott, Kenneth, 54
Allt, P., 77
Alpers, Paul J., 13, 14, 27
Alspach, R. K., 77
Anderson, Warren D., 54, 55
Andrews, Michael, 22
Anouilh, Jean, x
Antaeus, 21, 79
Antony, Mark, 19, 20, 22, 83
Aphrodite, 69 (see also Venus)
Apollinaire, Guillaume, 88
Apollo, 20, 23, 48–49, 57, 60, 63, 72
Apuleius, 26
Aratus, 7
Ariadne, 19, 83–84
Ariosto, Lodovico, 13
Arnold, Matthew, 35, 37, 50, 54*–58, 59, 62, 73, 82, 83, 85
Arthos, John, 15
Astraea, 6, 74
Athene, 52, 56, 72, 73
Attis, 63, 65
Auden, W. H., 95
Augustine, St., 88

Bacchus, x, xi, 5, 20, 25, 72 (see also Dionysus)
Bacon, Francis, 11, 26, 34, 44, 45

Bakeless, John, 16
Baker, Carlos, 42
Baldwin, Thomas W., 17, 18, 22, 100
Barber, C. L., 15
Barnard, Ellsworth, 42
Barrell, Joseph, 42
Bartlett, Phyllis B., 12
Bate, Walter J., 33, 34, 46
Battenhouse, Roy, 41
Baum, Paull F., 51, 54
Bayle, Pierre, 32–33
Beach, Joseph W., 38
Beaumont, Francis, 16, 84, 85
Benziger, James, 42, 46, 102
Berchorius, Petrus, 3
Berger, Harry, 13, 14, 27, 30
Blackmur, R. P., 67, 92
Blackstone, Bernard, 48
Blackwell, Thomas, 35–36
Blake, William, 34, 36, 68
Bliss, A. J., 23
Blissett, William, 28
Bloom, Harold, 41, 42, 102
Boas, George, 4
Boccaccio, Giovanni, 4
Bodkin, Maud, 1
Bogan, Louise, x
Bonjour, Adrien, 17
Bonnerot, Louis, 54
Born, L. K., 3, 100
Bostetter, E. E., 48
Bowra, Sir Maurice, 67, 103
Bradbrook, Muriel C., 16, 17, 100
Bradford, Curtis B., 71
Bridges, Robert, 66
Bronson, B. H., 33
Brooks, Cleanth, 67, 87, 97
Brooks, N. S., 13
Brower, Reuben A., 67, 71, 73, 76, 102
Brown, John R., 22
Browning, E. B., 63
Browning, Robert, 36, 55, 63
Buckley, Jerome H., 50

---

* An asterisk after a page number indicates a cluster of bibliographical references.